# Circular walks along
# the Sandstone Trail

*Walkers on the Sandstone Trail near Beeston Castle*

Circular walks along the
# Sandstone Trail

Carl Rogers

MARA BOOKS

First edition published in August 1994 by Mara Books, 22 Crosland Terrace, Helsby, Warrington, Cheshire, WA6 9LY.

Reprinted August 1995

Second edition published May 1998

Third edition published June 2002

Fourth edition published November 2005

ISBN 1 902512 10 3

Cover photos:     *Front: Peckforton Castle*
                  *Back: Peckforton Hills near Burwardsley*

## Acknowledgements
I would like to thank John Street, Sandstone Trail Ranger, David Morris, David George and Bob Nash for their help in revising and checking the route descriptions and providing additional photographs. I would also like to thank Cheshire County Council's Countryside Management Service for their support and sponsorship of the book.

British Library Cataloguing-in-publication data.
A catalogue for this book is available from the British Library.

Sketch maps based on out of copyright Ordnance Survey mapping

# Contents

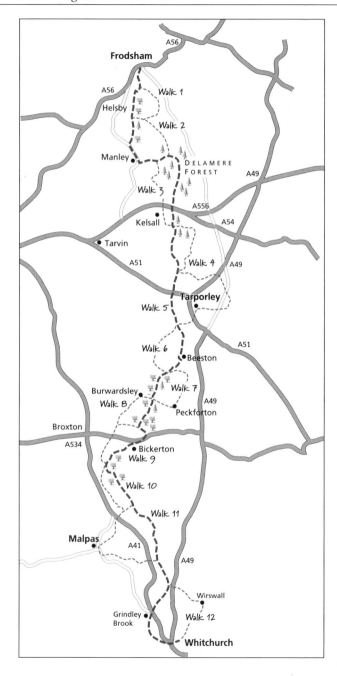

# Introduction

THE *Sandstone Trail* takes its name from the rolling sandstone ridge which forms one of Cheshire's most distinctive topographic features and provides a theme for the entire walk. This 'central ridge', presents a backbone of high ground which divides the flat lowland plains of the River Weaver to the east, and the broad Dee basin to the west.

The landscape along the ridge contrasts starkly with the rest of the county—mixed woodland exists on many of the escarpment slopes too steep for agriculture and small rocky outcrops provide numerous platforms from which broad views of the surrounding lowland (particularly west towards Wales) can be enjoyed.

The *Sandstone Trail* was one of the first recreational trails in the country and has become Cheshire's best known and most popular walking route. It was created by Cheshire County Council's Countryside and Recreation service to cater for more

*Looking north from Burwardsley to Beeston Castle*

*Bickerton and Larkton Hill from Raw Head*

serious walkers and the first 16 miles between Delamere and Duckington were officially opened at Easter in 1974.

Additional sections from Beacon Hill (above Frodsham) to Delamere and Duckington to Grindley Brook were added later, making a total length of 32 miles. The flight of steps leading down into Dunsdale Hollow near Overton Hill was named 'Baker's Dozen' in recognition of Jack Baker, one of the key individuals responsible for developing the Trail. In 2000 the Trail was extended again to link the towns of Frodsham and Whitchurch, making it more accessible by public transport and adding 3 miles to the length.

At Whitchurch the Trail joins the *Shropshire Way*, the *Marches Way*, the *South Cheshire Way* and *Bishop Bennet Way* and at Frodsham there are links with the *Delamere Way, Eddisbury Way, Baker Way, North Cheshire Way* and *Weaver Valley Way*.

# A brief history of the area

Like most of northern Britain, the topography of Cheshire has its origins in the movement and decline of ancient ice sheets during the last Ice Age. Surprising as this may seem, there are numerous remains from the Ice Age to be seen in Cheshire and many have had a fundamental influence on how the county has been settled.

At the peak of the last Ice Age, huge ice sheets are thought to have covered much of Britain including what is now Cheshire. Unlike highland glaciers, which originate in the mountains and flow down to the sea, the ice which covered Cheshire is thought to have come inland from the Irish Sea basin via the Mersey and Dee estuaries flowing over the county from north to south. This ice may well have been over 1,000 feet thick and originated in the mountains of Cumbria or southern Scotland. This is known from the many non-local boulders of all sizes to be found in Cheshire today and which were transported huge distances by the ice, then left behind when it retreated. They are known as 'glacial erratics' and the most common and easily recognised examples in Cheshire are the huge rounded granite boulders from Cumbria. An example can be seen in Frodsham Main Street, known locally as the 'Brook Stone', but similar examples will be seen frequently along the Trail, often gathered to field edges or built into walls.

When a glacier stops moving forward mounds of debris

*The large granite boulder which stands in the fields near Manley Common is a fine example of an 'erratic' and probably originated in the Lake District* accumulate at its leading edge. This is known as a moraine and the rolling hummocky landscape south Cheshire and northern Shropshire is a result of moraine debris left by the ice which flowed across Cheshire.

Meres are another common feature of Cheshire particularly in the southern half of the county. Many of these are thought to have originated as 'kettle holes' which form when a large block of ice melts, leaving a hollow which fills with the meltwater.

Another legacy of the ice is the layer of boulder clay covering much of the Cheshire Plain. This is the result of the ice grinding the local rock to a fine powder known as 'rock flower'. This is so fine that it becomes almost impervious to water resulting in poorly drained heavy soil little use for crop growing but able to support the rich grassland for which Cheshire is famous.

Another feature of central Cheshire is the deep layer of sand to be found around Delamere. This is thought to have been deposited by meltwater from the ice sheet as it retreated. The outflow came through the Mouldsworth Gap from the west and spread sand over a large area reaching east to Northwich and southeast to Winsford.

When the first settlers came to this area they would have found two contrasting landscapes created by the underlying soil. On the plains the heavy clay soils gave rise to dense impenetrable woodland with frequent swamps and mosses. The sandstone hills and sandy soils of Delamere on the other hand, would have been much drier under foot with more open woodland. This would have been far more attractive to early settlers, aiding both travel and hunting and evidence for the earliest periods of settlement, though slight, is confined almost exclusively to this area. It consists mainly of a handful of burial mounds identified near Oakmere, Kingswood and High Billinge at Utkinton, and a hoard of Bronze Age spearheads found at Broxton.

In later centuries however, with a change from hunting to agriculture, the central ridge became less attractive and by the time of the Norman Conquest the northern half, centred on what is now Delamere, was the most sparsely populated in the county. The light open woods were a haven for wildlife with deer, wild boar and even wolves roaming freely. The new Norman conquerors were noted for their love of hunting and chose this area for one of the King's royal hunting forests. But more about that later.

As far as early settlement is concerned it is not until the period immediately preceding the Roman occupation that any notable remains can be seen. These exist in the many Iron Age hill forts which enclose hilltops or promontories of high ground all along the central ridge. Those at Woodhouse Hill near Frodsham and Larkton Hill near Bickerton at the southern end of the Peckforton Hills are visited by the Trail, while a number lie close by—notably Eddisbury Hill, the largest hill fort in Cheshire.

These forts were built and occupied by Celts who began to move into Britain from the Continent around 500 BC. They were a restless warlike people and it is perhaps fitting that their most notable and enduring legacy is the many hill forts which can be

*The Iron Age hill fort on Eddisbury Hill*

seen across most of England and Wales today. All the Cheshire forts have been dated to the first century BC.

The Celts were organised into tribes with the Cornovii occupying what is now Cheshire and Shropshire. Archaeologists are unsure about just how the hill forts were used, but from excavations we know that the earth mounds (which would have been much higher than they are now) were topped by a timber palisade and in many cases were defended by outer ditches. There is evidence of hut circles within at least some of the Cheshire hill forts suggesting that they may have been more than just temporary dwellings or places to gather in times of trouble. When the Romans arrived these hilltop dwellings were abandoned and there are signs that some were destroyed by fire.

Throughout the Roman period Cheshire remained important as the site of the frontier fort at Chester (Deva). Watling Street, one of the main Roman highways, crosses the ridge at the Kelsall gap en-route to Chester. The *Sandstone Trail* crosses the line of Watling Street in Nettleford Wood about 300 yards before the busy A54 and there are some interesting remains of this road in the fields to the east of the wood where it makes its way towards Eddisbury Hill. Watling Street continued to be used as a road until the late eighteenth century.

When the Romans left Britain after three centuries of occupation the country as a whole deteriorated. The stone-built cities and villas fell into ruins and in some cases poorly constructed wooden structures were built within the magnificent buildings. Centuries later stories developed about the origin of such magnificent structures many claiming that they were built by gods. The road system also fell into disrepair and roads of the quality built by the Romans would not be seen again for over 1,800 years.

In many cases the British reverted back to the old tribal divisions with the result that when the next wave of invaders appeared, they were unable to present a united resistance with disastrous results. Irish invaders would have given the local tribes reason for concern initially, but this threat was dealt with by a warlord from the north of England who established himself in what is now North Wales and managed to halt the Irish colonisation.

It seems likely that Christianity reached Cheshire from the west during the early sixth century. Celtic 'saints' travelled throughout western Britain and Ireland setting up their churches. These early churches were known as *'llans'* and many Welsh villages have come to be named after their founder from this period. An example is Llangollen—the 'llan' or church of Collen who founded it. Cheshire must have had such preachers but most of their settlements and llans were swept away in the following centuries by pagan Saxon colonisers who gave settlements their own English names.

During the sixth century Cheshire was still firmly British, almost certainly under the control of the kingdom of Powys which could well have been centred on the already centuries old city of Chester. Powys embraced the earlier territory of the Cornovii and began in the previous century with King Cadell following what has come to be known as the 'Alleluliah Victory', fought against a heathen army (either Saxons or Scots from Ireland) near Mold.

In the following century more serious threats appeared as rivalries between expanding English kingdoms in the east spilled westwards. In 616 AD a Northumbrian king traversed the Pennines into what is now Cheshire and crossed the county (probably on what remained of Watling Street) to Chester where he faced the men of Powys on the banks of the River Dee. The exact site is unknown but it was close enough to the large Celtic abbey at Bangor-is-y-coed (Bangor-on-Dee), for over 1,000 monks to come to pray for a victory over the heathens.

The Celtic abbey at Bangor was one of the most important religious houses in the country at the time, far larger and grander than its sister abbey at Bangor in North Wales. The terrible defeat and the aftermath of the ensuing battle seems to have convinced the surviving monks that the abbey was in dangerous lands. It was abandoned and today even its location is unknown.

The Northumbrian king was Aethelfrith and he faced a weakened British force. Several local princes had not arrived by the time Aethelfrith's axe men cut into the British ranks. When the monks prayed out loud for a victory he ordered them to be cut down. Over 1,000 unarmed monks were slaughtered and the river was said to have run red for days.

After this defeat the British hold on the valuable Cheshire lands was lost and within a century much of the county was settled by the English. Ironically it was not the Northumbrians but the Mercians who moved into Cheshire from the southeast. Mercia was the eventual victor in a power struggle between Northumbria, Mercia and Gwynedd in North Wales.

So complete was this takeover that almost all the old Celtic names have been lost, with notable exceptions being river names and a handful of village names in Wirral. One advantage of this is that the new names give valuable clues to the phases of settlement and in some cases the condition of the land at the time of settlement. The earliest settlements can be identified by the name endings 'ing' or 'ham', such as Tushingham and Frodsham. These may represent the taking over of existing centres, with later phases being identified by the name ending 'ton', such as Beeston and Overton.

A later phase of settlement has been identified with the move to open up new, previously unused land which in Cheshire would have been forest. These settlements can be identified by the ending 'ley' which indicates a forest clearing and are common all along the central ridge. Examples are Tarporley, Manley, Alvanley, Kingsley, Burwardsley and Bickley.

By the end of the seventh century Mercians occupied nearly all of what is now Cheshire and from place names we know they continued the push west into Wales. But there they had trouble. The difficult terrain made things more difficult and the British were able to hold their own. A troubled borderland was the result. The Mercian King Offa dealt with the problem by building a great earthwork along his western frontier which still carries his name.

The Anglo-Saxons were not our last invaders. During the ninth and tenth centuries Norse-Irish raided all along western Britain and a number of place names in Wirral recall their settlements. They can be identified by name endings such as 'wall' (Heswall, Thingwall) and 'by' (West Kirby, Irby). The southernmost of the Wirral Norse settlements is Helsby, lying at the northern end of the central ridge below the crags of Helsby Hill.

Also during the tenth century came Danes from across the North Sea. They established themselves all along the east coast before pushing west. They eventually reached east Cheshire and are remembered in names containing the element 'hulme'.

The Mercians responded to this threat by building a line of fortresses from Runcorn south through Cheshire and into the Welsh Marches. One of these forts stood on Eddisbury Hill within the old Celtic hill fort and was built by Ethelfleda the daughter of Alfred the Great, known as 'the Lady of the Mercians'.

Saxon strongholds from this period can be identified by the name ending 'bury' which is derived from 'burh' meaning 'a fortified place'.

The Danes never conquered the whole of Britain, but in 1066 the entire kingdom fell to the Normans after their victory at Hastings. The Normans did not settle new lands and created few of their own settlements as previous invaders had, they simply took possession. Almost all the Anglo-Saxon land owners lost their lands. The last local Saxon earl was Edwin of Mercia. He was replaced by Hugh d' Avranches who became the first Norman earl of Chester. Earl Hugh was established at Chester by King William to carry the war west into Wales. Like the Saxons, the Normans had not been able to conquer Wales, so the king placed three powerful and ambitious warlords along the border to deal with the Welsh.

Chester became the base for launching attacks into North Wales and remained important to the English kings until the conquest of Wales by Edward I in the late thirteenth century. Throughout the eleventh and twelfth centuries, border conflict remained severe and the many motte and bailey castles whose mounds remain were built during this time. The majority lie to the west of the central ridge with a notable example at Malpas.

Another legacy from the Welsh wars is Beeston Castle. Built in 1220 by Randle de Blunderville Sixth Earl of Chester, it occupies a magnificent site on an isolated sandstone hilltop overlooking the Cheshire Plain. To the west there are uninterrupted views across the Dee basin into what would then have been enemy territory.

During the Middle Ages one of the most prominent features of central Cheshire were the two royal hunting forests of Mara and Mondrem which we have already mentioned. Royal hunting forests were created by the Normans to satisfy their taste for the hunt. These 'forests' were often centred on areas of natural woodland but were usually extended to include surrounding villages and farmland. We know from place names that much of central Cheshire was woodland during the Saxon settlement and this formed the heart of the new forest of Mara. Surrounding villages were also brought into the forest and placed under the restrictions of the harsh forest laws which were designed to protect both game animals and the vegetation which gave them cover.

The forest of Mara originally included all the land from the River Weaver to the River Dee. Its northern limit was the Mersey and it extended south almost to Tarporley. It is difficult to understand how the local population carried on their farming without breaking the forest laws, but punishments were often quite severe. In later centuries these laws were eased and agricultural activity gradually reduced the 'forest' area. Wolves are thought to have been eradicated from the Cheshire woods by the thirteenth or fourteenth century and no wild boar or deer

*Beeston Castle*

remained after the Civil War. The forest laws remained until 1812 when they were officially removed by Act of Parliament. The parishes of Delamere and Oakmere were created from the enclosed forest lands and the modern woods were planted on the land that remained.

The forest laws were enforced by Master Foresters whose job was to catch and punish offenders. They held a hunting horn as a sign of their office and were given valuable lands within the forest. The Done family held the office of Master Forester in Mara. Their seat was at Utkinton and their ancient hall still stands in the quiet lanes visited on walk 4.

The most famous member of the Done family was undoubtedly Sir John Done who received a knighthood at

Utkinton Hall in 1617 after entertaining the king, James I. James had spent the previous day hunting in Delamere and became only the second English monarch to do so in over four centuries. A portrait of Sir John Done dated 1619 shows him wearing the Delamere hunting horn carried as a sign of his authority.

Despite this proud image, it seems he was anything but satisfied with his office for in later years he tried to surrender it in exchange for a portion of land at the Old Pale near Eddisbury Hill. This was where the foresters held a hunting lodge known as the 'Chamber in the forest'. Little remains of this building today but William Webb, who passed through Delamere in 1620, describes it in this way: 'Upon highest hill of all and about the middest of the forest is seen a very delicate house, sufficient for the dwelling of the chief forester himself when it pleaseth him, and is called the Chamber in the Forest'. A few sandstone blocks on Eddisbury Hill close to the hill fort and adjacent to the old Roman road (Watling Street) are thought to be the remains of this building.

Although the forest has gone, its existence for so many centuries has had a major impact on the development of central Cheshire. In the heart of the old forest lands there are no ancient village centres or towns, and roads are, almost without exception, straight where they passed through previously unenclosed forest or heathland. This can be seen in the Delamere/Oakmere area where roads like the A49, A556 and A54 suddenly become almost completely straight. This is also apparent further north in the lanes and side roads around Kingswood and Newton near Frodsham.

Development has thus been centred away from these areas leaving central Cheshire quiet and rural. The landscape is primarily agricultural and the southern half of the county has probably changed little since the nineteenth century. The rich grasslands on either side of the sandstone ridge flourish on the heavy clay soils and support the dairy herds for which Cheshire is famous.

The highest parts of the ridge, on the other hand, are less suitable for agriculture and supported large areas of heath almost within living memory. Most are now wooded again; colonised by birch and remnants of oak.

This variable and interesting landscape, with its abundance of footpaths and bridleways, many originating as old forest roads, makes the central ridge one of Cheshire's most popular walking areas, with the largest numbers being attracted to the areas around Delamere and the Peckforton Hills.

*The dairy cattle for which Cheshire is famous*

*The Sandstone Trail between the two castles at Peckforton and Beeston*

# Walking the Sandstone Trail

The *Sandstone Trail* can be completed by strong walkers in a single day, but this would be something of an endurance test for most. A better option is to break the trail into sections—a two-day walk is ideal and there are a number of pubs, hotels and B&B houses in the central section around Beeston and Burwardsley providing accommodation. For a north-south walk the Burwardsley area is an ideal stop giving a shorter second day. For a south-north walk Tarporley is equally ideal.

This guide book has been written primarily with the more leisurely walker in mind and divides the trail into 12 circular walks all of which link with the previous and following route enabling two or more to be completed as circular walks. This means that by completing all the walks in the book you will have walked the entire *Sandstone Trail*. However, it can just as easily be used by those planning a north-south linear walk as explained below.

To complete the *Sandstone Trail* as a linear walk, either in one go or perhaps in two, three or more sections, the appropriate paragraphs in each chapter have been printed in <u>underlined text</u>. This will enable the walker to move easily through the relevant chapters as the walk progresses. For those completing the circular walks, the underlined text will identify the sections of each route which follow the *Sandstone Trail*.

## Further information

For details of all passenger travel and timetable information including the Sandstone Rambler bus service please contact Cheshire Traveline on 0870 6082608. Lines are open 8:00am - 8:00pm, every day except Christmas Day, Boxing Day and New Years Day.

The Trail uses both permissive routes and public rights of way. You should not experience any problems using the rights of way network but if you do, please report them to the PROW Maintenance and Enforcement Unit on: 01606 541801, or e-mail: countryside@cheshire.gov.uk

Cheshire County Council,
Countryside Management,
Phoenix House,
Clough Road,
Winsford,
Cheshire,
CW7 4BD

Further information about the Trail, including information on any temporary diversions, is available on line at: www.cheshire.gov.uk/countryside.

Details of accommodation and visitor attractions throughout Cheshire can be found at: www.visitcheshire.com.

# Frodsham

**Distance:** *6 miles*

**Section of the Sandstone Trail:** *Frodsham to The Ridgeway.*

**Start:** *Start the walk in the centre of Frodsham outside the 'Bear's Paw' pub where a stone monument marks the official start of the Trail. This is located at the junction of 'High Street', 'Main Street' and 'Church Street', Parking is available off 'Church Street'.*
*Grid ref. 517 778 (Ordnance Survey Landranger 117, Explorer 267).*

**Local facilities:** *Frodsham – Local shops, WC, car parks, pubs; Overton – two pubs: 'Ring o' Bells' and 'Bulls Head'.*

## The walk

**1.** <u>Walk up 'Church Street' passing 'Eddisbury Square', 'Kingsway' and 'Churchfield Road' on the right. A little further on turn right up steps onto a signed footpath between gardens. Follow this up to Overton Church.</u>

*There has been a church on this site since at least Norman times. The present building contains portions of a Norman nave and cloister with some ancient stonework which may predate this.*

*The manor of Frodsham was held by Edwin the last Saxon Earl of Mercia immediately before the Norman Conquest and is rumoured to have been part of the lands granted to Dafydd the brother of Llywelyn, the last independent prince of Wales, by Edward I in the thirteenth century. This was the reward for treacherously aiding Edward in his war against Llywelyn. After later taking sides with his brother against Edward, he was captured and mercilessly hung drawn and quartered as a traitor at Shrewsbury.*

Walk ahead past the 'Ring o' Bells' and the 'Bull's Head' and where the road bends left turn right along 'Middle Walk'. As you enter the woods bear left on the signed footpath and at the next junction turn sharp left. At a T junction turn sharp right onto a traversing path and just before you emerge from the trees near the top of the hill bear left to arrive at the war memorial.

Follow the signed footpath beyond the memorial along the top of the hill with the hotel up to your left.

At a line of small crags bear right as signed down to a traversing path. Keep left along this walking below the crags which become higher further along. Pass a small quarry on the

*The start of the Sandstone Trail outside 'The Bear's Paw', Frodsham*

*Helsby Hill from above Dunsdale Hollow*

left, continuing ahead to reach the deep depression of 'Dunsdale Hollow'.

*The rock steps which descend the cliff here are known locally as 'Jacob's Ladder',—a local beauty spot in bygone days and often the goal of a traditional Sunday walk.*

Make your way down the flight of wooden steps just beyond Jacob's Ladder ('Baker's Dozen') to a junction of paths directly below the cliffs.

Ignore the broad path on the right here, instead, bear left on the well worn path which crosses the back of the hollow before rising again over a small rock step. Continue with the golf course to your left at first, then with trees on both sides.

At a rock platform on the right giving a view out towards Helsby Hill, bear left on the signed rising path over Woodhouse Hill. The path skirts the highest point up to the right which is crowned by the earthworks of an Iron Age hill fort (not visible from the path).

*This relatively small enclosure is one of several hill forts which are to be found on the high ground of the central ridge. They were built by Celts of the Cornovii tribe in the years before the Roman occupation.*

With fields ahead bear right along the edge of the woods following the obvious footpath as it bends left to a junction. Turn right here and follow a distinct sandy path overhung by trees. Lower down, the path becomes a sunken lane with high banks on both sides.

*Overton and its ancient Church*

<u>For the *Sandstone Trail* follow this sandy lane to the road, where there is a caravan site on the left. Turn left and continue from point 1, route 2.</u>

**2.** For the circular route turn left into a small field just before the caravan site on the left (immediately before a large pond also on the left). Cross the field and turn right along a short track. At the entrance to the next field turn left over a stile to follow the footpath through an attractive little valley. Follow the valley until it narrows and make a short rise. Go ahead through a small field to Manley Road.

Cross the road and follow the lane opposite. At the top of the rise bear left and in about 400 yards turn left again onto a sandy track. Follow the track to a junction with a tarmac lane and turn left. Descend another sandy track to a group of houses (known as Shepherds Houses) on Manley Road.

*The distinctive straight lines taken by the roads and bridleways in this area contrast sharply with the winding lanes found elsewhere in Cheshire. This is a remnant from earlier days when much of this area was open common. It is hard to imagine now, but just a few hundred years ago all the land around Shepherds Houses and south to Delamere Forest was open heath with occasional woods—a landscape similar to that of the New Forest today. When the common was enclosed around the turn of the nineteenth century the roads and lanes were formalised, but with no fields or dwellings to avoid they followed the long straight lines which we see today.*

**3.** Turn right and follow the road for about 150 yards before turning left over a stile onto a signed footpath. Bear half-right through the field and cross a farm track. An enclosed footpath now takes you beside the golf course to emerge in Simon's Lane.

Turn left along the lane and in about 150 yards, turn right down the drive to 'Overhill Cottage'. Where the drive bears left to the cottage, continue straight ahead between gardens to cross the drive to 'Heathercliffe', a large country hotel on the left. Follow the footpath straight ahead, soon with sloping ground and wide views on your right .

At the road ('Bellemonte Road') turn right down the hill and at the 'Bellemonte Hotel' bear left across the small car park taking the signed footpath on the right. This leads down steps to meet the road again. Turn left and follow the road to Overton Church where you can retrace the outward journey.

# Manley Common

**Distance:** *6¹/₄ miles*

**Section of the Sandstone Trail:** *The Ridgeway to Manley Common*

**Start:** *There is limited parking available on the verge opposite the track to Snidley Moor and adjacent to Ridgeway Wood. This lies part way along a pretty lane known as 'The Ridgeway'.*
*Grid ref. 508 748 (Ordnance Survey Landranger 117, Explorer 267).*

**Local facilities:** *Nothing directly on the route. Pubs nearby at* **Alvanley** *–'White Lion' and* **Mouldsworth** *–'The Goshawk'.*

## The walk

**1.** Walk a few yards up the lane to where steps on the right lead into 'Ridgeway Wood'. Follow the path down wooden steps and bear left to walk beside a stream on the right. After leaving the wood by a footbridge over the stream, keep left in the following fields to reach Commonside Lane.

Cross the lane and take the rising path opposite which soon levels out below the wooded slope of Alvanley Cliff and above 'Cliff Farm' down on the right. After a few fields the way is blocked by 'Austerson Old Hall'. Turn right here as signed and look for a stile in the field corner. Walk ahead through fields to a quiet lane. Looking back you will get views of the Hall.

*Although the Hall appears to have been sitting here for centuries, it is in fact a fairly recent addition to the local landscape. It was brought from the hamlet of Austerson, near Nantwich, by a local architect and reassembled here in the 1980s.*

**2.** <u>Opposite, a short field path leads to Manley Road below the wooded hillside of Simmond's Hill. Turn right here and at the T junction bear left up the hill.</u>

*Where the road levels there are good view out to the right across the Dee basin towards Wales in clear conditions. If the light is right you can often see the distant silhouette of Chester Cathedral.*

<u>Pass Manley primary school and church. About 300 yards beyond the church, turn left through a kissing gate and follow the path along the field edge. Climb the stile in the far corner and turn right through a small field to meet the road again. Turn left here and walk along the lane to Manley Common.</u>

**3.** <u>Where the lane bears left by houses, take the signed *Sandstone*</u>

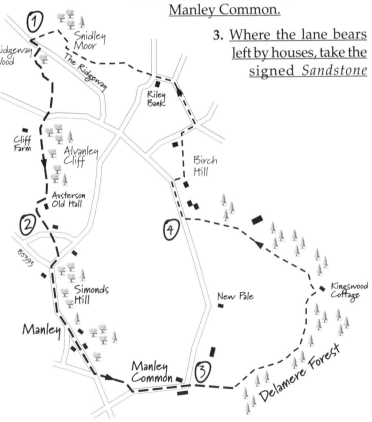

*Trail* path straight ahead which leads into the forestry plantations at Delamere. For the *Sandstone Trail* continue from point 5, route 3.

*The open land to the left is known as the New Pale and is a relic from Delamere's earlier history as a hunting forest. The forest was created by the Normans to protect game for the king's hunt and relied on strict forest laws enforced by the Master Foresters. They had powers to impose severe penalties on anyone found in breach of the forest laws, which included not only the killing of game animals, but also the harming of vegetation which gave them cover. To a population who lived entirely by agricultural means, this must have been a severe hardship as whole villages, like Alvanley and Manley, lay within the forest bounds.*

*In later centuries it became increasingly difficult to protect the game as forest lands gave way to agriculture, as a result, forest enclosures were built in an attempt to preserve the deer. The New Pale is thought to have originated in this way and dates from about 1617. The oval shape of the enclosure can still be picked out on modern large scale maps.*

*Deer were finally wiped out in Delamere during the Civil War and although plans were made to reintroduce them, it never happened.*

*In 1812 the forest laws were officially removed by an Act of Parliament and the modern plantations at Delamere were established on a small portion of the land. The remainder was turned into agricultural land and two new parishes were formed, Delamere and Oakmere.*

As you enter the forest turn left onto a broad forest path. Follow this undulating path keeping left at a T junction and at the next junction (an angled crosspaths) turn left again. The next section of the route follows the *Delamere Way* and is frequently waymarked.

Follow the broad path, soon with fields on the left. At a gap in the trees, turn right with the path and walk below overhead cables. At the next junction turn left onto a forest road and after

*Austerson Old Hall*

a few yards turn left again at a T junction. Follow the forest road past 'Kingswood Cottage' and where it bears right a little further on, take the path straight ahead on the bend. Take the first path on the left and follow this, soon with fields on the left, to the road ignoring a crossing path (*Eddisbury Way*) partway along.

**4.** Turn right at the road and in about 200 yards, bear right into 'Birch Hill' just before the bend. Pass bungalows on the right and go through the gate of 'Birch Hill Cottage' to a stile and field path on the left. Walk along the field edge and farm track to a quiet lane beside a farm. Turn right here and bear left at the crossroads. At the next junction bear left down the hill to 'Manley

Road'. Opposite, a stile and field path lead down into a picturesque little valley.

Follow the path along base of the valley and at the lower end, just before a large pond, cross the stile and turn right along a short track. In the following field bear left along the hedge to a kissing gate which leads onto a sandy track. Turn left now and follow the track back to 'The Ridgeway' to complete the walk.

*Delamere Forest*

*Looking towards Woodhouse Hill, Overton Hill and Frodsham from Helsby*

*Manley Common*

*Manley Common*

*Pale Heights and Delamere Forest*

*Sandstone Trail near Nettleford Wood, Delamere*

*Wharton's Lock, on the Shropshire Union Canal*

*Cottages near Beeston*

*Sandstone Trail near Beeston Castle*

*Peckforton Castle*

*Beeston Castle*

*Looking down to Harthill from Raw Head*

*Peckforton*

*Near the summit of Larkton Hill*

*Old St Chad's, Tushingham*

*Shropshire Union Canal near Grindley Brook*

# Delamere Forest

**Distance:** *8¹/₄ miles.*

**Section of the Sandstone Trail:** *Manley Common to Primrosehill Wood.*

**Start:** *Begin the walk at Barns Bridge Gates car park situated on Ashton Road in Delamere Forest.*
*Grid ref. 542 716 (Ordnance Survey Landranger 117, Explorer 267).*

**Local facilities: Delamere Forest** – *occasional refreshment vans at Barns Bridge Gates and along Ashton Road. Cafe, toilets and gift shop at **Delamere Visitor Centre** (just off the trail near Eddisbury Lodge). **Kelsall** – pubs: 'Th'ouse at top', 'The Olive Tree' and 'The Oak'.*

## The walk

**1.** Beside the car park entrance a broad forest path signed for the *Sandstone Trail* leads away from the road. Follow this path keeping straight ahead at a prominent junction of forest tracks. Where the forest track bears sharp right, continue straight ahead on a footpath to cross a railway bridge. Beyond the bridge a dip and rise lead onto a narrow footpath beside 'Eddisbury Lodge'. At a T junction with an unsurfaced lane turn left and after a few yards bear right (as signed for the *Sandstone Trail*) onto a rising track between fields.

At the top of the rise enter Nettleford Wood by a large gate. An alternative route for the *Sandstone Trail* has been created here which climbs up onto Pale Heights and gives wide views in clear conditions. For this option turn left through a kissing gate immediately (signed 'alternative route') and follow the path up

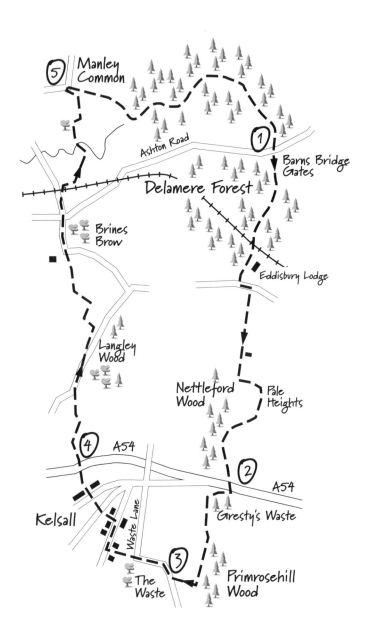

5 Manley Common

Ashton Road

1

Barns Bridge Gates

Delamere Forest

Brines Brow

Eddisbury Lodge

Langley Wood

Nettleford Wood

Pale Heights

4 A54

Kelsall

Waste Lane

2

A54

Gresty's Waste

3

The Waste

Primrosehill Wood

a sloping field through an area of new planting and towards the aerials on the summit of Pale Heights. At a gravel track turn right and in about 50 yards bear right on a path through a gap in the hedge. Follow the gravel path ahead with wide views west towards Wales and later east to the Pennines in clear conditions. After the next gap in the hedge bear right to enter Nettleford Wood and join the original *Sandstone Trail* route again by the carved wooden sign. Alternatively, reach this point by continuing ahead on the broad path as you enter Nettleford Wood.

Turn left and follow the prominent footpath to the busy A54.

**2.** Cross the road (very fast traffic!) and descend a flight of wooden steps to cross a footbridge. Bear right up the bank and after a short climb follow the path between fields along an avenue of trees to enter Primrosehill Wood, part of the Delamere plantations.

Follow the path left then, in about 20 yards, bear right up hill with the main path. Ignore minor footpaths which join from the left, until the main signed path turns sharp left. For the *Sandstone Trail* turn left here with the main path and at the bottom of the slope bear left on a forest track. Continue from point 2, Route 4.

For the circular walk don't turn left with the *Sandstone Trail,* instead keep ahead on a narrower footpath. At a T junction with a prominent forest road turn right and rise to the lane at King's Gate car park.

**3.** Turn right along the lane (Waste Lane) to The Waste, a small area of scrub and ponds on the left. Immediately after this, where the lane turns sharp right, take the signed field path straight ahead through the kissing gate. Keep to the field edge at first, then join an enclosed footpath which descends between gardens to emerge in a small cul-de-sac ('Elizabeth Close').

*Kelsall is a large village attractively laid out at varying levels on the steep slopes of the central ridge which give it a bird's eye view of the Cheshire Plain. It developed around one of the few gaps in these steep escarpment slopes, a feature exploited as early as Roman times. Watling*

*Street, the Roman road which linked the settlements of Deva (Chester) and Condate (Northwich), passed through here and in later centuries when the turnpikes were built, a similar line was taken.*

Continue to 'Quarry Lane' and turn right. After about 300 yards take a narrow footpath on the left (after 'The Nook') which drops to a stream before rising to the road. Opposite, a second footpath passes between gardens and leads to 'Old Coach Road'. Turn right here then immediately left into 'Brooms Lane'. Where the lane bears left, follow the signed footpath straight ahead and cross the busy A54.

**4.** The following section to the junction with the *Sandstone Trail* at Manley Common is part of the *Eddisbury Way* and is waymarked here and there. Cut straight through a fruit growing area following a prominent track (ignore left fork). Pass through two gaps in the conifer hedges used as wind breaks, cross a track near a pond on the left, then, keeping more or less straight ahead, walk with the hedge on your right until you are forced to turn either left or right at a T junction. Turn left here and look for a stile and steps in the corner which lead into sloping fields on the right. Walk diagonally down the field to a gate which takes you into a quiet lane.

Turn right along the lane and after about 500 yards look for a signed footpath on the left. Pass through a gap in the hedge and wall, then turn right and walk parallel to the road. Turn left along the second conifer hedge and where four hedges meet, turn right (keeping the hedge on your right). Bear left in the corner and look for a gap in the hedge below a solitary oak tree amongst the conifers. Cross the stile and bear half-left through the field aiming for the opposite corner and passing a powerline post (with waymarker disc). Just before a gateway turn right over a stile and pass through an area of abandoned farm machinery and vehicles. After a second stile, turn left along the field edge to reach the road.

Turn left and follow the lane past 'Brines Brow Picnic Area'

*Delamere Forest*

on the right to a crossroads. Continue straight ahead here, signposted 'Manley, Frodsham'. After about 200 yards bear right just before the railway bridge and follow a track which passes beneath the arches of the bridge. Beyond, turn right and walk parallel to the railway for 100 yards or so (to a point where the railway on the right enters a small cutting). Turn half-left through the centre of the field to a stile in the far hedge. (At the time of writing a direct route between the bridge arch and the stile in the hedge is being walked but this is not strictly on the line of the right of way.)

Walk directly through the following field to the far corner

where you will find a stile and footbridge over the stream hidden amongst the trees. Cross the bridge, rise directly up the bank, and turn left to follow the edge of the field parallel to the stream. In the corner of the field turn right and rise up the field edge to a stile in the top corner. Cross the stile and follow a short path through the trees before turning right over a second stile. Walk along the field edge with fine views to the right. After about 100 yards turn left over a stile beside a gate and walk ahead up the field turning left in the corner to the houses at Manley Common.

**5.** Turn sharp right (rejoin the *Sandstone Trail* here) and follow a wide footpath on the opposite side of the hedge, signed to 'Delamere Forest'.

As you enter the woods continue straight ahead on the prominent descending path. At a T junction turn left and follow the broad forest road ignoring a left fork by the stream. At the top of a rise (about 400 yards) bear right, then immediately left onto a sandy path with young trees on both sides. At the next junction go ahead on the broad forest road.

*These modern plantations, with their regimented even rows, are all that remain of the ancient forest of Delamere, created by the Normans to provide exclusive hunting grounds for the crown and preserved for over 700 years by strict forest laws.*

*The primary function of the forest laws was to protect game animals and the vegetation which gave them cover. This meant that the agricultural needs of the local population took second place and those tempted to disobey risked severe punishment. This must have placed many under extreme hardship as several villages lay within the forest bounds.*

*Delamere originally consisted of the twin forests of Mara, on which the modern plantations are centred, and Mondrem which lay to the south and east of what is now the A49. At their greatest extent these forests included all the land and villages between the River Weaver and the River Gowy, and extended south from the River Mersey to the outskirts of Nantwich.*

*The villages around its edge must always have exerted pressure on the forest lands and over the centuries its area became greatly reduced, mainly through the practice of 'assarting' or the ploughing of forest land for agriculture.*

*Despite this, much of the forest of Mara remained until the mid-eighteenth century when a series of enclosure orders were granted to the surrounding parishes allowing them to divide up the portion of their lands which came within the forest area. In the following century an Act of Parliament was passed which allowed the enclosure of Delamere itself. This happened in 1812 and resulted in the creation of two new parishes, Delamere and Oakmere. The land that remained was retained by the crown and planted with conifers to form the modern plantations.*

*Of Mondrem only Little Budworth Common survives, although there is still much evidence for both forests in the local landscape. If you look at a modern map you will notice that in the heart of the old forest area there is a complete absence of ancient village centres—all the older settlements lie around what was then the forest edge.*

*Evidence of enclosure can also be seen in the many straight roads which previously crossed open forest or heath. For example, look at the way in which the line of the A49 between Cuddington and Cotebrook contrasts with that further north or south. The A54 between Kelsall and Winsford is another example. On large scale maps you will also notice that the enclosed lands are composed of large fields with straight boundaries which contrast sharply with the smaller irregular field patterns of the surrounding areas.*

<u>In about 400 yards and just before the track bends left, bear right. After a short rise follow the sandy track ahead along the edge of the woods with fields on the left. Keep right at a fork and continue to the road at Barns Bridge Gates car park. For the</u> *Sandstone Trail* <u>continue from points 1 & 2, route 3.</u>

# Primrosehill Wood

### Distance: 7³/₄ miles.

**Section of the Sandstone Trail:** *Primrosehill Wood to Fishers Green.*

**Start:** *Begin the walk at King's Gate in 'Waste Lane', Kelsall.
Grid ref. 535 678 (Ordnance Survey Landranger 117, Explorer 267).*

**Local facilities: Summertrees Tearooms** – *closed Mondays and Fridays* **Kelsall** – *pubs: 'Th'ouse at top', 'The Olive Tree' and 'The Oak'.*

## The walk

**1.** Follow the broad forest road which descends into the woods (ignore the path signed to Nettleford Wood on the left in about 200 yards) to join the *Sandstone Trail* at a junction of paths (about 500 yards).

*In the trees to the left of the path here is a curious sandstone gorge known as Urchin's Kitchen. Rock features such as this are rare in Cheshire and all manner of fanciful tales must have been told over the centuries to explain its existence. The reality though is perhaps more of a surprise than any folk tale. It is thought to have formed under a vast ice sheet at the height of the last Ice Age. Under tremendous pressure from a covering of over 1,000 feet of ice, water found a natural weakness in the rock and as this became enlarged a mixture of rock debris and sand was swept in a spiral motion creating the undercut walls which can be seen today.*

*Only part of the gorge is now visible, with at least half buried and it could be as much as 70 feet deep. An interpretation panel nearby gives more information.*

**2.** Bear right with the main forest track and in another 100 yards or so turn right onto a narrower signed footpath. At the edge of the woods bear left and after about 200 yards, wooden steps and a kissing gate lead into sloping fields on the right. Turn right here and at the top of the rise cross into fields on the right continuing on the opposite side of the hedge to a lane with 'Summertrees' tearooms on the right.

Continue straight ahead at the lane and after about 30 yards bear right onto an enclosed sandy footpath which runs along the top of Willington Hill for about ¾ mile.

**3.** At the lane (Willington Lane) turn left and after about 300 yards, enter fields once more on the right (*Sandstone Trail* sign). Keep beside the hedge in the first field, then cross a stile in the top corner and bear left along the upper edge of a large sloping field with wide open views of the Peckforton Hills and the Cheshire Plain to the right.

At a crossing track turn right and make a short steep descent to enter a field again. Continue ahead through the field until you are forced to turn right in the bottom corner. Walk beside a stream until a footbridge allows you to pass into fields on the left. Turn right now and continue around the field edge to a lane (Wood Lane).

Opposite, the *Sandstone Trail* continues along an old farm track known as Old Gypsy Lane. Where the lane runs into fields, turn left over a stile and after about 100 yards, a second stile takes you to the right of Oxpasture Wood. After two more stiles by a small pond bear half-right through the centre of a large field to join a farm track near a house on the left (Fishers Green). For the *Sandstone Trail* bear right along a farm track (Gullet Lane) and continue from point 2, route 5.

**4.** For the circular walk bear left and follow the lane ahead past Fishersgreen Farm (ignore a lane on the right 'Ridge Hill') to a crossroads with 'Utkinton Road' (almost ½ mile). Continue straight ahead along 'Hall Lane' to Utkinton Hall on the right.

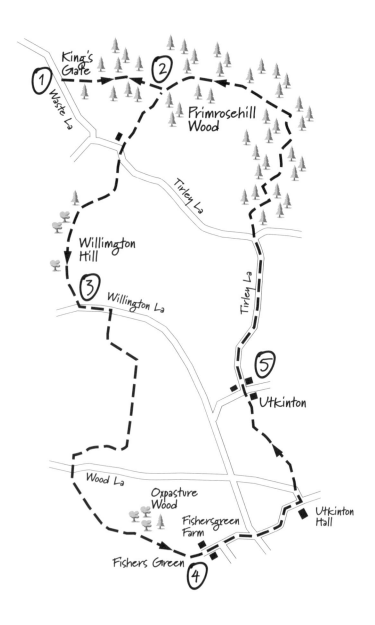

*Utkinton Hall is the ancient seat of the Done family who held the office of Master Forester in nearby Delamere for almost five centuries. Henry was the first Master Forester, a title he inherited when he married Joan Kingsley, the heiress, in 1244. Sixteen Dones followed him of which four were knighted. The family line ended in 1662 with Mary Done, grand-daughter of Sir John Done.*

*Dones from Utkinton Hall have played their part in several major battles which helped to shape British history. At the Battle of Agincourt in 1415, John Done fought alongside Cheshire archers, while Sir John Done, the eighth Master Forester, perished along with other Cheshire gentry at the Battle of Blore Heath in 1459.*

*The Master Forester's primary role was to preserve 'beasts of the chase' and the vegetation which gave them cover in the king's forest. The royal hunting forests were a Norman idea and the Master Forester was rather like a modern day game keeper, except that in the eleventh century, when the forests were created, such game would have been highly coveted by the local population. In addition, the woods were home to numerous outlaws, a group of desperate men who, with no right of audience in a court of law, could be killed or injured by the foresters with no questions asked. As a result, there were frequent violent confrontations. Records tell of one such encounter in 1351 when Richard Done was pardoned for causing the death of Robert Cosyn who resisted arrest for killing deer in Delamere.*

*In the eleventh and twelfth centuries the foresters had the power of life and death in the woods and could execute felons on the spot for such crimes as being 'caught in the woods with a dog on a lead' or 'having a drawn bow or a bloody hand'.*

*The severe forest laws were eased during the reign of King John and from this time on, the practice of 'assarting' or the ploughing of forest land for agriculture became common. It was also about this time (early 1300s) that wolves finally disappeared from Delamere, probably as a result of the shrinking forest area and increasing agricultural activity.*

*The most famous Done was undoubtedly Sir John Done who received a knighthood at Utkinton Hall on the 25th August 1617 from James I.*

James had spent the previous day hunting in Delamere and became only the second English monarch to do so in over four centuries. A portrait of Sir John Done dated 1619 shows him wearing the Delamere hunting horn carried as a sign of his authority.

Despite this proud image, it seems he was anything but satisfied with his office for in later years he tried to surrender it in exchange for a portion of land at the Old Pale near Eddisbury Hill. This was where the foresters held a hunting lodge known as the 'Chamber in the forest'. Little remains of this building today but William Webb, who passed through Delamere in 1620, describes it in this way, 'Upon highest hill of all and about the middest of the forest is seen a very delicate house, sufficient for the dwelling of the chief forester himself when it pleaseth him, and is called the Chamber in the Forest'. A few sandstone blocks on Eddisbury Hill adjacent to the old hill fort are thought to be the remains of this building.

Sir John Done died in 1629 and a year later his son died childless which ended the male line. The Forestership passed to Sir John's eldest daughter, although this was unsuccessfully contested by another branch of the family, the Dones of Flaxyards near Tarporley. His properties, including the hall, were eventually divided between his four daughters.

Turn left into a lane (Smithy Lane, not named) opposite the Hall and after about 75 yards a stile and gate on the right indicate the field path to Utkinton. Follow a faint farm track beside the hedge at first, then bear left with a fence on the right to a stile and steps in the top corner of the field. In the next field, keep right along the field edge and immediately after a second stile, cut diagonally-left through the centre of the field (aiming for new houses ahead) and drop down the bank to a kissing gate and pond which leads onto a well used footpath. Turn right here and rise up steps to 'Northgate', a narrow access road with houses on either side. Follow 'Northgate' to a crossroads in the centre of Utkinton by the school.

**5.** Continue straight ahead following 'Tirley Lane' for about ¾ mile.

At a T junction with Primrosehill Wood ahead go straight ahead into the trees following a prominent forest track. Bend right with this track and after a descent where the track turns sharp left, go straight ahead on the bend following a faint path (ignore a path on the right). This path becomes more pronounced as you continue to descend. Continue ahead crossing a wet area and following the path as it rises again.

At the top of the rise turn left at a T junction and at a junction of paths and forest tracks turn sharp right onto a broad forest track. Follow this track as it descends to make a sharp left turn. Continue on this track and take the first obvious path on the right (about 500 yards from the sharp bend) which follows the edge of the plantations with fields on the right.

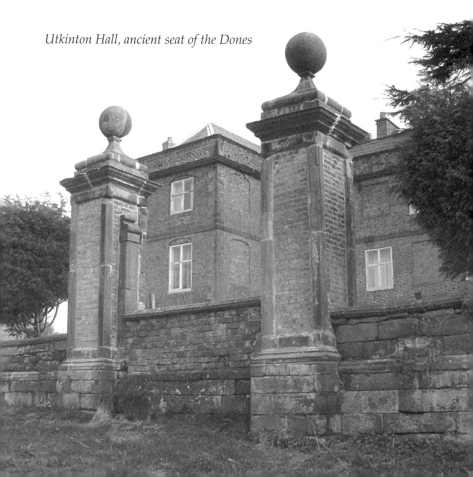

*Utkinton Hall, ancient seat of the Dones*

*Over to the right you will see the flat topped Eddisbury Hill, site of an Iron Age hill fort and centre of the Old Pale, a forest enclosure dating from the fourteenth century. It seems likely that it was originally created to prevent the escape of deer although in later centuries parts were ploughed for agriculture.*

*As mentioned already, Eddisbury Hill is known to be the site of the 'Chamber in the forest', referred to by Sir John Done and William Webb. The strangely isolated location of this building can be explained by the fact that until the mid-eighteenth century the main route through Delamere followed the line of Watling Street, the old Roman road which linked Northwich and Chester. Unlike the modern route, this took a direct line over the shoulder of Eddisbury Hill and it was here at the highest point in the forest that the 'Chamber' was located.*

After a rise, turn right at a T junction and follow the main forest road back to King's Gate car park.

*The Rising Sun Inn, Tarporley*

# Tarporley

**Distance:** *7½ miles.*

**Section of the Sandstone Trail:** *Fishers Green to Crib Lane.*

**Start:** *Begin the walk at the public car park located behind the 'Rising Sun Inn' in Tarporley High Street.*
*Grid ref. 553 628 (Ordnance Survey Landranger 117, Explorer 267).*

**Local facilities:** *Tarporley – local shops, post office and pubs – 'Rising Sun Inn', 'The Swan Inn', 'The Foresters'.*

## The walk

**1.** Turn right out of the car park along 'High Street' and just before the 'Swan Inn' cross the road and turn left down 'Park Road'. Pass 'Tarporley War Memorial Hospital' and where the road turns right take the signed footpath straight ahead. Cross the stile and go ahead along the left-hand fence line.

*Tarporley is a sought-after commuter village in the very heart of the Cheshire countryside. The fine Georgian terraces which line the High Street date from a period of prosperity in the late eighteenth century and although there is nothing here of great antiquity the village centre has retained a strong rural character despite a number of modern developments.*

*For centuries Tarporley was associated with nearby Delamere Forest and originally lay within the extensive woodland which covered vast areas of Cheshire before the Norman Conquest. This is known from the name ending 'ley' —a common place name element in central Cheshire. It is derived from the Saxon 'leah' and referred to a settlement cleared from forest lands. Other examples locally include: Alvanley, Kingsley and Manley.*

At the lane turn left for about 70 yards before turning right into a rough gravel driveway. At the end of the driveway pass 'Garden Cottage' crossing the stile ahead to enter the golf course. At the first road turn right and follow it passing the clubhouse on your right. Ignore the driveway to the left adjacent to the clubhouse, instead continue ahead until the road turns right. Go ahead here as indicated by a fingerpost ('Sapling Lane').

Take a direct line across the golf course aiming just to the right of a group of pines on the skyline. Pass to the right of the pines and join a gravel path which descends into a small hollow or depression. Shortly bear left to a stile by a gate. Go over the stile and follow an enclosed path down to a lane (Sapling Lane). Turn right and walk along the lane into the little village of Eaton.

Go ahead at the cross for a few yards and turn left into 'Lightfoot Lane'.

**2.** 'Lightfoot Lane' starts as a tarmac lane but soon deteriorates into a sunken lane, then a footpath as it rises gradually onto Luddington Hill. At a gravel track turn right as signed and continue on the enclosed footpath until the golf course on the left ends. Turn left over a stile here and follow the right way along the right-hand edge of the golf course to the A49.

Turn right and walk along the road for about 270 yards passing 'Broadway Farmhouse'. Cross over and take the signed footpath on the left immediately after this. Descend steps and walk down the left-hand field edge to a stile in the lower left corner. In the following field cross a footbridge over a stream on the left and turn right along the bank. Cross a stile into the field on the left and turn right along the field edge. In the corner of the field there is a stile—don't cross this, instead turn left along the field edge and continue to the lane.

Turn left along the lane and follow this to the rambling farmhouse of Utkinton Hall (see the previous chapter for notes on the Hall's history) on the left where the lane swings right. Go straight ahead here and the next crossroads go ahead again ('Fishers Green'). Ignore a lane on the left in about 400 yards ('Ridge Hill') continuing ahead to the end of the lane.

**3.** After 'Fishersgreen Farm' and the final house on the right, the lane becomes unsurfaced and it is here we join the *Sandstone Trail*. Follow a farm track which swings left and eventually runs into fields. At the end of the track go through a kissing gate and keep ahead by woods on the left. In the bottom corner turn right with the path to a second kissing gate. Go through the gate and turn left  to reach the busy A51.

Opposite, and to the left, enter fields again by a signed path adjacent to a farm track. Walk ahead through four small fields before joining an enclosed footpath. Turn right along the path

*Eaton Cross*

and follow it to eventually cross a footbridge and enter fields
again by a kissing gate. Bear left along the hedge at first, then
where the hedge veers left, keep ahead through the following
fields with Beeston Castle directly ahead.

*Here we are in the heart of Cheshire's dairy country. The heavy clay
soils which cover most of the plain are damp and difficult to plough
and are given over almost exclusively to pasture. This traditional use
gave rise to Cheshire's famous cheese, made from the milk of the
distinctive black and white Friesian cattle.*

50

Stiles separate the fields and there are two footbridges. The second footbridge leads into the final two fields before 'Crib Lane'. To continue on the *Sandstone Trail*, bear left along the hedge to a stile in the corner. Go over the stile and continue from walk 6, point 4.

**4.** For the circular route don't cross the final stile, instead look for a stile on the left a few yards before this (after the second footbridge). Go over the stile and head straight across the field aiming for farm buildings on the skyline. Cross a stile and sleeper bridge and continue across the following field to enter a lane by a stile in the far right-hand hedge line.

Turn left along the lane and about 70 yards after houses on the left go over a stile by a gate also on the left. Keep along the right-hand hedge to a stile in the corner. Cross this stile and the following small field and farm track to enter a field by two stiles. Aim for an aerial passing it on the left. Soon Tarporley church comes into view. Head for this and partway along the hedge on the left go over a stile and turn right along the opposite side of the hedge. In the lower corner of the field cross the stile and the busy bypass and ascend the steps opposite to enter fields again. Go ahead along the field edge and look for a stile down to the left. Cross this and bear half-right towards Tarporley church.

An old kissing gate leads into the cemetery. Walk through the cemetery and out into 'High Street' where a left turn will take you back to the 'Rising Sun Inn' to complete the walk.

# Beeston Castle

**Distance:** 5¹/₂ *miles.*

**Section of Sandstone Trail:** *Crib Lane to Beeston Castle.*

**Start:** *There is a private car park at Beeston Castle which can be used by walkers but a 'donation' is payable in the castle shop. Please do not use the car park without checking in the shop as it is locked when the castle is closed. If you would like to check availability and opening times the phone number is (01829) 260464. An alternative start could be made from the 'Shady Oak' (point 3).*
*Grid ref. 540 591 (Ordnance Survey Landranger 117, Explorer 257).*

**Local facilities:** *Pub: 'Shady Oak'.*

## The walk

**1.** From the castle car park (opposite the gatehouse) turn left along the lane for a few yards and bear right on the *Sandstone Trail* beside the wall enclosing the castle grounds. Where the path forks, bear left away from the wall through a small conifer plantation to a quiet lane. Take the path opposite and a little to the left beside the garden of a cottage. Follow the path through the centre of a large field, cross a wooden footbridge over a small stream and continue ahead through a second large field. About halfway up the field take the signed *Sandstone Trail* on the right and cut diagonally through the following field to a lane.

*Across the valley you will see the crumbling ruins of Beeston Castle perched on its conical hill and viewing the Cheshire Plain as it has done for over seven centuries. It is built on the most ideal of sites—a steep isolated hill with a commanding view of the surrounding plain.*

*Throughout the walk its distinctive outline will rarely be out of view. The castle dates from 1220 and was built by Randle de Blunderville, Sixth Earl of Chester. For the next three centuries it passed in and out of royal ownership until, by the early sixteenth century, it was*

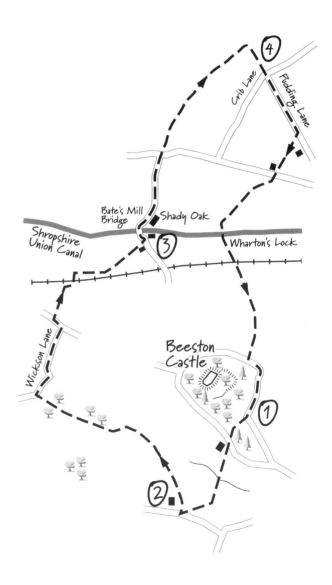

*Beeston Castle from Wharton's Lock on the Shropshire Union Canal*

abandoned and began to fall into ruins. In the following century however, enough of the defences remained to give cover to a band of Parliamentarians for over nine months. In December of 1645 Royalist troops ousted them before fleeing after their defeat at the Battle of Rowton Moor, near Chester. Parliament ordered the partial destruction of the defences in the following year and the castle has been little more than a ruin ever since.

According to legend, Richard II hid valuable treasure in the 400-foot deep well in the upper keep during the fourteenth century, although searches made in 1842 and 1935 failed to find any sign of the royal hoard.

**2.** Turn sharp right onto a farm track immediately and follow the track to a T junction where a stile immediately ahead indicates the continuation of the right of way. Cut through the centre of the following field to a stile, then bear left in the next field to a stile in the far fence. Go ahead now following the right of way along the right-hand field edge.

Ignore a signed footpath on the right partway down the field, instead, continue ahead towards a small wood at the bottom of the field. A stile and wooden footbridge take you into the trees and a stile leads into a small field. Go ahead to 'Wickson Lane'.

Turn right and follow the lane to a T junction with a grand view of Beeston Castle to the right. Turn left here and after about 30 yards turn right over a stile into fields. Walk ahead through the field and bear right to a low bridge which leads under the railway. Go under the bridge and turn right to walk parallel to the railway. About halfway along the field turn half-left through the centre of the field aiming for a house.

**3.** A short footpath to the left of the house leads to the lane. Turn left here and follow the lane over the canal passing the 'Shady Oak' public house. Carry on up the lane to a T junction.

A stile straight ahead indicates the start of the field path which you should now follow. Go over the stile and cut through the centre of the first field to a stile, then in the second field, aim for the top right-hand corner where a footbridge leads over a ditch. Bear diagonally-right through the following field past a small pond to a second footbridge. Go ahead to a stile in the far right-hand corner of the field. Cross the stile and turn right to join the *Sandstone Trail* in the corner of the field.

**4.** Turn right over the stile in the corner and <u>keep beside the</u> <u>hedge until you are almost at 'Crib Lane'. Bear left over a stile</u> <u>here and enter the lane a few yards further on. Turn right, then</u> <u>left into 'Pudding Lane'. Walk along the lane and just before a</u> <u>small cottage on the right, turn right through a kissing gate</u> <u>cutting through three small fields with Beeston Castle directly</u> <u>ahead. Cross 'Huxley Lane' and follow the path opposite which</u> <u>descends through a large field to Wharton's Lock on the</u> <u>Shropshire Union Canal.</u>

*This waterway, along with most of Cheshire's canals, was built in the latter half of the eighteenth century to provide a link between the industries of the midlands and the Mersey ports. Less than a century later the advent of the railways brought a steady decline and many canals fell into disrepair. This has been largely halted in recent years by a growth in the holiday trade. The Shropshire Union Canal now forms part of a network of canals which run throughout the county known as the Cheshire Ring.*

<u>Cross the canal and a small footbridge over the infant River</u> <u>Gowy. A track now leads beneath the railway before rising gently</u> <u>through fields to join a quiet lane below Beeston Castle. Turn</u> <u>left and follow the lane back to the car park by the castle. For the</u> *Sandstone Trail* <u>continue from point 1, route 7.</u>

# *Peckforton*

**Distance:** *5¹/₂ miles*

**Section of Sandstone Trail:** *Beeston Castle to Burwardsley.*

**Start:** *As for route 6.*

**Local facilities: *Burwardsley*** – *'The Pheasant Inn' and café at the Cheshire Workshops (both just off the route at point 2.).*

## The walk

**1.** From the castle car park (opposite the gatehouse) turn left along the lane for a few yards and bear right on the *Sandstone Trail* beside the wall enclosing the castle grounds. Where the path forks, bear left away from the wall through a small conifer plantation to a quiet lane. Take the path opposite and a little to the left beside the garden of a cottage. Follow the path through the centre of a large field, cross a wooden footbridge over a small stream and continue ahead through a second large field. About halfway up the field take the signed *Sandstone Trail* on the right and cut diagonally through the following field to the lane by stone houses. Turn right along the lane and after about 200 yards bear left on the signed path into the woods of the Peckforton Estate. Follow a well established track through the woods rising steadily.

At a junction of paths near a cottage on the right continue ahead and about 450 yards further on, bear diagonally-left onto a path which climbs the hillside (signed to 'Bulkeley Hill'). At the top of the rise bear right (ignore the path ahead) and walk beside woods at first, then through a small field with wide views

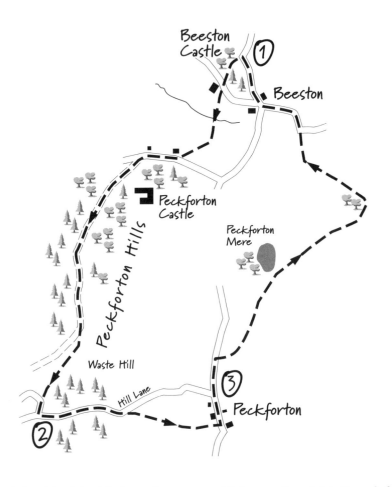

of the Cheshire Plain and across to Wales on the right. Turn left at the lane and at the next junction turn left again. For the *Sandstone Trail* continue from point 2, route 8.

**2.** For the circular walk, follow the lane—which soon becomes unsurfaced—until it begins to descend towards Peckforton and immediately beyond a small sandstone bridge over the lane, bear right into fields on the signed path.

*The bridge is known locally as the 'Haunted Bridge' and was built in the 1850s to take carriages from the recently built Peckforton Castle to the gatehouse at Peckforton Gap.*

Follow the edge of the woods for a few yards, then bear left down through the centre of a large sloping field. Two isolated oaks mark the line of the right of way which continues beside a fence to a stile in the field corner. Keep to the right of a small quarry and look for a stile close to a large, ancient oak beneath whose branches John Wesley is reputed to have preached. Follow the path through an area of young trees and bear left at 'Bank Cottages' to the road in the centre of Peckforton village.

*Walking through this village with its tiny cottages is like stepping back in time, yet things have not always been so quiet here. In the early*

*Laundry Cottage and its curious statue*

*1800s there were nearly twice as many properties as there are today. One of the cottages which still stands, was previously a public house called 'The White Horse', while a water mill which has now been demolished, stood near the River Gowy in fields to the right.*

*Several of the cottages show signs of having had repairs or additions when Peckforton Castle was being built in the 1850s. The most outstanding example is undoubtedly the stone elephant with a castle on its back which stands twelve feet high in the garden of 'Laundry Cottage'.*

*This remarkable statue was carved in 1859 by John Watson who was employed at Peckforton Castle as a stone mason. Originally intended as a beehive, it was cut from four separate pieces of stone and had a tiny pane of glass in every window. It originally stood in the garden of a cottage further up the hillside but was moved to its present location when the cottage was demolished in 1890.*

*The rather curious subject of the carving may be explained by the fact that the Corbett family, who owned Peckforton until 1626, had an elephant with a castle on its back featured in their coat of arms.*

**3.** Turn left and walk along the lane.

Just beyond a pair of cottages on the right, look for a fingerpost and a gap in the hedge (opposite stone steps on the left). Go right through the gap keeping the hedge on your right until you come to a fingerpost in the field corner. Ignore this, instead go left following the hedgerow on your right. Carry on around the field edge to a metal gate in the far corner. Go through the gate, cross a farm track and the stile opposite. Cut through the centre of the field now to a footbridge, then go half-left in the following field to a second footbridge with Peckforton Mere encircled by trees on your left.

*Until the early 1800s the land around Peckforton Mere, was a wild, waterlogged waste known as Beeston Moss. Today, drainage schemes have reduced it to a small pool surrounded by farmland.*

The next field is very large and the right of way passes just to the right of centre. At the top of a slight rise in the field, walk towards the left-hand end of a red-bricked bungalow in the distance to a stile beside a wooden horse jump (can be difficult to find). In the next field bear right and head for a stile to the right of a small wood and continue beside the trees. At the corner of the wood turn left and follow the woodland edge to another stile in the corner.

*Rising from the trees on the northern end of the Peckforton Hills are the turrets and battlements of Peckforton Castle, built in 1850 for the first Lord Tollemache by Anthony Salvin the Victorian architect. It was designed in the style of a Norman Fortress, common enough at the time but unlike elsewhere, Peckforton is not just a facade of turrets and battlements. It has inner and outer wards with gatehouses and a great hall open to the roof. Because of this it has been used as the setting for several television productions, notably the 1991 Robin Hood film.*

Walk ahead through the centre of the next field (aim just to the right of Peckforton Castle) to a footbridge over a drainage ditch. Bear half-left across a small field to cross a farm track by two stiles. In the following field walk half-left again to a large pond. Turn sharp right here and walk through the centre of a large field towards a farm (Brook Farm). A stile to the right of the farm takes you onto a short track which leads to the road. Turn left along the road keeping left at the next junction and take the right fork by a distinctive black and white cottage. In another 30 yards turn right and follow the lane back to the castle car park to complete the walk.

# Burwardsley

**Distance:** *5 miles.*

**Section of Sandstone Trail:** *Burwardsley to Raw Head.*

**Start:** *Start at the Cheshire Workshops in Higher Burwardsley where refreshments are available. There are two car parks here the outer one is for walkers, the inner car park should be left for visitors to the workshops. Grid ref. 523 565 (Ordnance Survey Landranger 117, Explorer 257).*

**Local facilities:** *Higher Burwardsley: 'The Pheasant Inn' and café at the Cheshire Workshops at the start of the walk.*

## The walk

**1.** Turn left out of the car park, then bear immediately right and continue straight ahead at a small crossroads up 'Rock Lane'. Follow the narrow rising lane ignoring a left fork, to join the *Sandstone Trail* at the top of the rise where a second lane joins from the left.

**2.** About 50 yards further on turn right through a kissing gate and follow the footpath along the field edge. A kissing gate in the far corner leads onto an enclosed path beside the pine woods of the Peckforton Estate. After this, keep ahead through the following fields to a lane. Turn left along the lane and shortly you will reach the gatehouse at Peckforton Gap.

*Peckforton Castle was built in 1850 for the first Lord Tollemache by Anthony Salvin, the Victorian architect responsible for a number of Cheshire country houses. This one is quite different though, built in the style of a Norman fortress, it uses local stone and has been used as the setting for several television productions.*

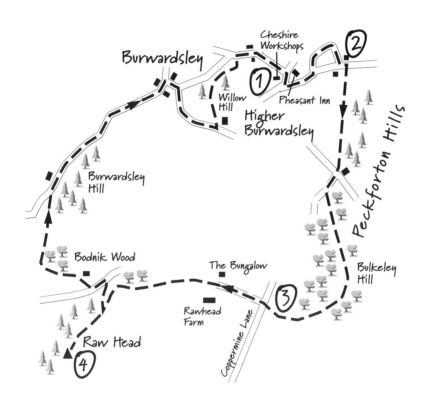

Turn right along the sandy lane opposite the gatehouse. Walk along the lane for about 150 yards, then turn left up a flight of stone steps which lead into 'Bulkeley Hill Wood'. Follow the rising path through the trees. As the angle eases the path swings left to follow the edge of the steep escarpment which falls dramatically to the flat farmland around the village of Bulkeley.

*In the winter months an absence of foliage on the trees allows an extensive view which takes in much of the central Cheshire Plain laid*

*Looking through the trees from Bulkeley Hill*

out like a vast green carpet. Nearer at hand this patch work of fields and hedgerows ends abruptly at the foot of these steep tree-clad slopes.

This contrast between the plain and the hills has always existed. In prehistoric times when the plain was thickly wooded and poorly drained, the hills provided a lighter drier environment with thinner tree cover and easily worked soils. This made them more attractive to Bronze Age and Iron Age settlers whose earthworks still crown several hilltops in the vicinity. In later centuries, when settlers drained and cultivated the plain, the hills became extensive heathland used to graze livestock. Today, a lack of grazing has allowed the woods to regenerate.

On the steep eastern face you will see tramlines used in the construction of a water pipeline to one of the nearby pumping stations.

*These access vast reservoirs of fresh water which collect against the impenetrable clay soils of the plain. Further evidence of this can be seen in the many springs which are particularly common on the lower slopes.*

Continue along the edge of the hill passing through a gap in metal railings with an underground reservoir enclosed by a fence to your right. Make a drop now to eventually leave the woods by a kissing gate beside a larger gate. Turn half-right and cut through the centre of a field to 'Coppermines Lane'.

**3.** Go ahead along the farm road opposite until it bears left to 'Rawhead Farm'. Continue straight ahead on a footpath for about 50 yards before bearing left through a kissing gate. This path hugs the edge of the hillside with occasional views out to the right along the hills to Beeston Castle.

*As you walk along the path look for a damp outcrop below to the right which holds a well and weeping stone known locally as the 'Droppingstone' (dripping stone). This is one of many fresh water springs which are quite common along these hills. Also common are caves which have been cut into the soft sandstone, possibly by those in search of fine sand for scouring cottage floors.*

*Local folklore has endowed the caves with all manner of fanciful legends. Outlaws, brigands and hermits are all reputed to have occupied them and they have been given names to match: Bloody Bones Cave, Queen's Parlour, Musket's Hole and Mad Allen's Hole.*

The path eventually leads above small crags with fields on the left to the summit rocks of Raw Head (marked by an Ordnance Survey triangulation pillar), at 227 metres the highest point on the *Sandstone Trail*. For the *Sandstone Trail* continue from point 3, route 9.

*As you would expect the view on a clear day from all along this hillside is extensive (although trees are beginning to encroach particularly around the summit itself) and takes in much of south Cheshire, the hills of North Wales and the Pennines to the east. Further south the Shropshire hills are often visible against a foreground of rolling wooded hills which shelter the tiny village of Brown Knowl.*

*Looking west from near the summit of Raw Head*

**4.** Retrace your steps from the summit for about 300 yards and turn left onto a path which drops steeply into the trees. Descend through a young conifer plantation and at the road turn left. After about 150 yards (just before a signed path on the left) a footpath drops steeply through trees on the right to enter a field by a stile. Walk ahead through the field with a cottage on the right and enter woods by a stile (Bodnik Wood). Go ahead through the trees to a stile leading into fields. Cross the stile and turn right immediately over a second stile. Bear half-left through the following large field to a stile below a large oak tree (aim to the left of a stone house on the hillside above). Cross the stile and walk along the top edge of the following field to meet the lane below the wooded slope of Burwardsley Hill. Turn right and follow the lane for about ¹/₂ mile.

Take the first turning on the right which leads into Burwardsley village and after about 50 yards bear right again ('Sarra Lane'). Where the lane forks at the end of houses on the right, keep left. Follow the lane and after a dip and rise look for a stile on the left just before a small cottage ('Quarry Cottage'), signposted 'Willow Hill'. Turn left over the stile and follow the path through a garden, then up to a stile and along the top of the wooded hillside before dropping to the lane. Turn right here and follow the lane up to 'The Pheasant Inn' at the top of the hill. Turn right here to the car park to complete the walk.

*The Pheasant Inn, Higher Burwardsley*

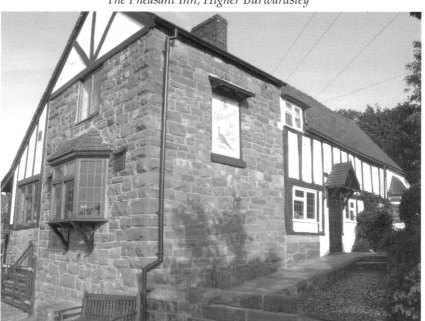

# Raw Head

**Distance:** *5¹/₂ miles.*

**Section of Sandstone Trail:** *Raw Head to Larkton Hill.*

**Start:** *There is a large car park with a Sandstone Trail information board adjacent to 'The Copper Mine' pub on the A534 at Brown Knowl. At the time of writing, walkers are welcome to park here, but remember this is not a public car park, parking is only at the landlord's permission. Grid ref. 499 542 (Ordnance Survey Landranger 117, Explorer 257)*

**Local facilities:** **Brown Knowl** – *'The Copper Mine' and 'The Durham Heifer' pubs (just off the route on the A 534) .*

## The walk

**1.** Turn left out of the car park and walk up 'Sherrington Lane'. At the end of the lane turn right and follow the road to the A534. Turn left here and follow the road for about 100 yards before crossing over to enter fields by a kissing gate (immediately after 'Fullersmoor Farm'). Walk ahead along the field edge to cross a stile and footbridge in the corner. After the bridge go straight ahead to a stile, then ahead up the field to a stile partway up the left-hand hedge. Cross the stile and turn right up the sloping field beside the fence towards the conifers of Park Wood. The right of way runs beside Park Wood and eventually curves right into the little village of Harthill with its ancient church.

**2.** Cross the road and follow 'Garden Lane', which is almost opposite and to the right of the school. At the end of the lane enter a large sloping field. Go ahead up the field to Bodnik Wood on the skyline. At the edge of the trees bear left to the corner where there are two stiles. Go over the right-hand stile into the wood. Follow the path ahead through the trees leaving the wood near a stile with a small cottage on the left. Walk ahead again through the field to a stile, then rise through a small beech wood to a quiet lane. Turn left up the lane and look for a signed path on the right which indicates the footpath to Raw Head.

Rise steeply through a young conifer plantation to emerge high up on the exposed hillside overlooking the green vale through which you have just walked. Turn right here and follow the *Sandstone Trail* to the summit of Raw Head.

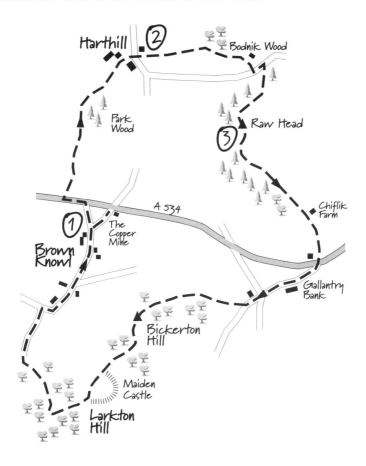

*At 227 metres this is the highest point in Cheshire west of the Pennines and gives a commanding view of the surrounding countryside, although this is in danger of being obscured by recent tree growth. On a clear day you will be able to see the Wrekin and Shropshire Hills to the south, while the Clwydian Range line the western horizon. Away to the north the hills around Helsby and Frodsham are just visible with the massive tower of Liverpool's Anglican cathedral on the skyline.*

*Nearer at hand, the River Dee winds through peaceful green pastures —the subject of bitter dispute between English and Welsh during the Dark Ages. Today all is peace and quiet, although remnants of a line of moat and bailey castles remind us of more troubled times.*

**3.** From the summit the path continues along the top of the slope before descending a flight of steps to pass a number of crumbling sandstone crags.

*There are numerous breaks in the trees along this hillside allowing wide views into the green vale below. This break in the hills is thought to have been used by a medieval salt road which followed the approximate line of the present A534 and linked the salt producing town of Nantwich to the ford at Farndon and the route into Wales. This particular road was known as 'Walesmon's Way'.*

The path eventually leaves the edge of the hillside to run beside woods on the right. Lower down join the drive to 'Chiflik Farm' and follow this to the A534 at Gallantry Bank.

*Gallantry Bank was originally known as 'Gallows Tree Bank', after the body of a murderer was gibbeted here in 1640.*

Cross the road and follow the lane almost opposite signed to 'Whitchurch'. At the crossroads go straight ahead ('Goldford Lane') and immediately beyond Bickerton Church, bear right onto Bickerton Hill, signed for the *Sandstone Trail*. This section of the *Sandstone Trail* is well used and a broad path has been worn into the sandy soil.

*The trees thin out near the summit of the hill and again you are treated to a bird's eye view of the surrounding countryside. Prominent in this panorama is the tiny village of Brown Knowl where the walk*

*Near the summit of Larkton Hill*

*began, along with the conifers of Park Wood and the high sandstone ridge at Raw Head.*

*Below, hidden on the overgrown hillside lies the curiously named 'Mad Allen's Hole'. This man-made cave obtained its unusual name from a hermit who was said to have lived here towards the close of the eighteenth century. The story goes that he chose the life of a hermit after he was refused the hand of the girl he loved by her parents.*

*Having sold all his possessions, he lived for a number of years in one of the caves on Raw Head until his solitary existence was disturbed by unwanted visitors. Presumably the cave on Bickerton Hill was better concealed as he seems to have remained here until his death at the age of about 70.*

<u>Beyond the highest point (Kitty memorial) the path veers away from the edge and shortly you come to a junction with a</u>

track and a fingerpost. Turn right as signed for the *Sandstone Trail* and at a second junction, also with a fingerpost, continue ahead on a slightly narrower footpath.

*Larkton Hill is crowned by the remains of Maiden Castle, an Iron Age hill fort dating from the first century BC. It is the southern-most of a group of hill forts which line Cheshire's central ridge, all but two occupying summit locations such as this. These may seem strange locations today but remember that in prehistoric times what is now the tame cultivated landscape of the plain was primarily a wild, thickly wooded and poorly drained moss. This often impenetrable jungle made the central ridge, with its lighter well drained soil and thinner tree cover extremely attractive to early settlers.*

*The tribe thought to have built Cheshire's hill forts were the Cornovii who had their capital at Wroxeter in Shropshire. Being a reasonably peaceful tribe they were easily subdued by the Romans and as a result their hill forts show few signs of conflict.*

*To the casual observer the low banks which remain give little indication of what the fort originally looked like, but excavations by Liverpool University in 1934-35 and again in 1962 revealed the defences to have been quite extensive. Two curving ramparts enclose an area of 1.5 acres, while a line of low crags defended the north-western perimeter. The inner mound was found to have been up to 12 feet high and supported by drystone walling. This would have been topped by a wooden palisade.*

*The main entrance lay on the north-east side and consisted of an inturned passage which originally had a cobbled surface. It seems likely that a pair of large gates defended the entrance.*

*Of dwellings within the enclosure surprisingly little remains, however, quarrying activity and the removal of sand in recent centuries may be to blame for this. From excavations elsewhere it seems likely that a number of circular huts would have been built within the enclosure. These would have had wattle and daub walls with thatched or turf roofs.*

*The name Maiden Castle has attracted a host of romantic interpretations over the centuries, but J McNeil Dodgson, in* 'The Place Names of Cheshire' *tells us that it is derived from the Old English 'Maegden' which means 'virgin' or 'untaken' (untaken fort).*

*This hill is one of Cheshire's few remaining heathlands and has been designated a Site of Special Scientific Interest (SSSI). In recent years a lack of grazing has resulted in an increase of invasive birch and scrub which is threatening the heather and bilberry. Moves are now being taken to halt and reverse this process by the reintroduction of grazing animals.*

Immediately after the castle bank bear right on a path down the front of the hill (ignore a left fork partway down) to a little sandy col at a junction of paths amongst the trees (for the *Sandstone Trail* turn left here and drop to a *Sandstone Trail* information board where a sign directs you left along the foot of Larkton Hill. Continue from point 1, route 10).

To complete the circular walk, turn right and follow the well worn footpath down through the trees. After a large wooden gate, go ahead past a small sports field on the right and in 100 yards or so turn right down an access track ('Sandy Lane'). At the end of the lane turn right and follow the road through the village of Brown Knowl. Bear right at 'Sherrington Lane' and return to the car park at 'The Copper Mine'.

# Hampton Heath

**Distance:** *5 miles.*

**Section of Sandstone Trail:** *Larkton Hill to Hampton Post.*

**Start:** *There is a small car park on National Trust land at the head of a cul-de-sac leading up towards Larkton Hill at Duckington. This can be reached by turning south off the A534 near the 'Durham Heifer' along 'Old Coach Road'. Turn left in about 1½ miles immediately before a thatched cottage on the right.*
*Grid ref: 494 525 (Ordnance Survey Landranger 117, Explorer 257).*

**Local facilities:** *Pubs – 'The Market House', on the A41 at Hampton Heath (half a mile off the route).*

## The walk

**1.** Turn left out of the entrance to the little car park and follow the sandy lane left to the *Sandstone Trail* information board. Turn right here and <u>follow the signed path along the edge of woods with fields on the right.</u>

<u>After about ½ mile, turn right through a kissing gate and walk down a sloping field to a quiet lane with Larkton Hall directly ahead.</u>

*It is here that the Sandstone Trail finally turns its back on the sandstone hills which have been its theme for over 20 miles. Between here and Whitchurch lie the quiet green pastures of Cheshire's dairy country. The heavy clay soils which make ploughing difficult are ideal for the rich green grasslands which are such a distinctive feature of the Cheshire Plain.*

74

*Equally distinctive are the black and white Friesian cattle whose numbers were decimated by the foot and mouth outbreak in the late 1960s. Cheshire fared better in the 2001 outbreak with just a handful of cases within the county.*

<u>Continue along the track opposite to Larkton Hall. About 100 yards before the Hall, where a concrete track starts, turn right through a kissing gate and walk diagonally through the field to a kissing gate in the opposite corner. Walk ahead in the next field to a kissing gate which leads onto the access drive. Turn right down the drive to the lane.</u>

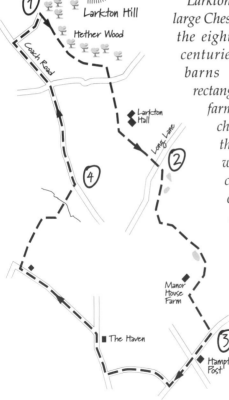

*Larkton Hall is typical of many large Cheshire dairy farms built in the eighteenth and nineteenth centuries. The farmhouse and barns are built around a rectangular yard and, like many farms in this area, there is a cheese parlour adjacent to the main house. Cheshire was once famous for its cheese making although only one or two farms still make cheese in the traditional way.*

<u>2. A stile immediately opposite leads into fields once more. Bear half-right beside ponds to a stile in the far fence. Cut through the centre of the following field in</u>

*Looking back to Bickerton and Larkton Hill from Hampton Post*

the direction of a large farm in the distance. A second stile in the fence leads into a smaller field and a stile and footbridge take you over a ditch. Keep left beside the hedge until you can pass into fields on the left just before a large pond. Continue, now with the hedge on your right, through two fields and in the corner of the second field turn right over a stile near Manor House Farm, also on the right. Walk through a small field to a stile, turn left and follow the field edge to a quiet lane.

**3.** Turn right and follow the lane to Hampton Post crossroads. For the *Sandstone Trail* turn left on the signed path about 200 yards before the crossroads. Continue from point 3, route 11.

*This crossroads was once on the main London to Chester Turnpike before what is now the A41 was built lower down on the plain in 1821. This cut out the hilly section between No Man's Heath and Broxton further north. Parts of the lane are still known as 'Old Coach Road'.*

76

Continue straight ahead at the crossroads and take the first lane on the right. Follow the lane to a T junction, turn right and after about 200 yards bear left into a narrow lane. Just before a sharp left-hand bend turn right into fields again at a kissing gate. Walk ahead to a stile to the right of a pond. Keep left along the field edge to a stile by a gate. Go over this and continue along the field edge until a stile in the hedge allows you to pass into fields on the left. Bear right around the field edge to a stile in the bottom corner then cut through the centre of the next field to a stile which leads into a lane and turn left.

**4.** Follow the lane for about ³/₄ mile (straight ahead at a crossroads) and turn right into the lane which rises gently towards the wooded slope of Larkton Hill and the National Trust car park to complete the walk.

# Malpas

**Distance:** *8½ miles.*

**Section of Sandstone Trail:** *Hampton Post to Old St Chad's Church.*

**Start:** *There is a small car park in the centre of Malpas off 'High Street' close to the Post Office.*
*Grid ref. 488 473 (Ordnance Survey Landranger 117, Explorer 257).*
**Local facilities:** *Malpas – local shops, pubs, café and post office.*

## The walk

**1.** Turn left out of the car park and along 'High Street' down to the Cross in the centre of Malpas. Turn left into 'Well Street' opposite the 'Crown Hotel'. On the outskirts of Malpas bear left at a fork in the road. At a second fork bear left again and in 100 yards or so turn right on a signed path, initially down a drive, then ahead along a green lane. Where the track swings left into a farm keep ahead on a footpath enclosed by hedges. At the end of the path continue ahead through two fields.

At the end of the second field, arrows on a post indicate a footpath to the right and left—turn right here and head for a stile in the corner of the field between ponds. Go over the stile and turn left immediately. Walk through two fields close to the hedge on the left to a quiet lane with a farm to your right. Opposite, the signed footpath continues along a farm track. After a stile at the bottom of the field turn left and follow the line of a disused railway (crossed by a number of gates) for about 400 yards to a stile. Beyond the stile turn right and pass through the remaining fields to a lane. Turn right and follow the lane to the crossroads with the A41.

Follow the lane opposite ('Cholmondeley Road') to a crossroads at Hampton Post, previously a junction on the old London to Chester turnpike. Continue ahead ('Shay Lane') for about 200 yards to the path signed for the *Sandstone Trail* on the right and turn right.

**2.** Follow the path ahead through several fields with distant views of the south Pennines to your left. As you near stables ahead, bear half-left as signed through a paddock to a stile which leads into a quiet lane. Walk down the drive directly opposite to 'Middle House' and immediately before the gates, turn left through a small metal gate. Walk beside the fence/hedge on the right to a small metal gate in the lower corner. In the next field walk past outbuildings on the right and look for a stile in the

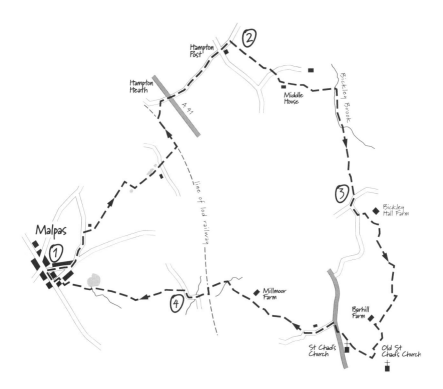

bottom corner of the field. Cut diagonally-left through the following field to a stile and footbridge below a large tree. Keep left along the field edge, then across the open field to where a footbridge to the left of a farm bridge leads over Bickley Brook.

Turn right now past the farm bridge and keep beside the brook. Cross a footbridge over a side ditch, then a footbridge back over the main brook again. Bear right to a stile a few yards away and turn left along the field edge. After a gradual rise through a large field to a stile in the far fence, continue straight ahead still rising, shortly with the hedge on your right. At the top of the rise pass a solitary oak and keep straight ahead to where a gate beside a pond leads onto 'Bickley Road'.

**3.** Turn right along the road and take the first turning on the left, signposted, 'Whitchurch 5'. About 150 yards along the lane bear left over a stile by a gate and as you approach Bickley Hall look for a stile in the hedge on the right. Cut through the centre of the following field (with the farm to your left), to a stile in the far corner. Cross the stile and bear right along the hedge to a second stile on the right. Go over the stile and bear half- left to the outside corner of a field on the left, then cut diagonally-left through a larger field to a metal kissing gate in the bottom hedge. Walk ahead for about 50 yards then turn right over a stile and follow the right-hand field edge to a stile in the corner. After the stile join a farm track ahead which leads to Barhill Farm.

*Several Roman Roads are known to have passed close to here and in 1812 an important find was made in the field to your right by a local farmhand. It was a Roman military discharge certificate which has come to be known as the 'Malpas Diploma' and consists of two bronze tablets nine inches by six held together by hinges. It was issued in AD 103 to a Spaniard by the name of Reburrus for 25 years service and granted him and his descendants Roman citizenship.*

*It seems likely that the certificate was lost as Reburrus travelled along one of the roads between Whitchurch and either Chester or Wilderspool near Warrington.*

*Approaching Old St Chad's Church*

Walk through the farmyard and turn left over a stile almost opposite the farmhouse. Walk beside the fence to a stile in the corner, go over the stile and turn left in the next field to climb another stile in the corner. Bear right around a hollow and head for a stile in the hedge ahead. After the stile keep ahead with the hedge on your left to a stile and fingerpost in the corner. For the *Sandstone Trail* turn left over the stile and walk across the field to Old St. Chad's Church. Continue from point 2, route 12.

For the circular walk don't go over the stile, instead, turn sharp right and cut through the centre of the field to modern St. Chad's Church.

Go through the right-hand kissing gate in the far corner and

*Cottages and church, Malpas*

continue ahead through the following field to a stile onto a farm access road. Turn left and cross the road (A41). Walk right along the footpath to a quiet lane on the left, signposted, 'Bradley 1'. About 350 yards along the lane a stile on the right leads into fields once more. The next section of the walk is part of the *'Marches Way'* which runs between Chester and Whitchurch.

Keep to the right-hand hedge/fence line until you pass a farm on the right (Millmoor Farm). Cross to the other side of the fence by a stile on the right here beside a gate and continue ahead. A little further on another stile leads you back to the left-hand side of the fence again. At the bottom of the field a footbridge leads over a brook and a second stile a few yards away on the left takes you into a large field. Walk half-left through the centre of the field (aiming to the left of a large tree in the far hedge).

Go over a stile in the hedge (this is on the line of an old railway whose embankment can be seen to the left) and turn left along the hedge to a stile in the corner of the field. Go over the stile and bear right down the bank to cross a footbridge over the stream. Keep right again to a stile in the fence. Go right for a few yards then contour around the field leftwards to enter a lane by a stile.

**4.** Turn right along the lane. At the top of a rise (about 300 yards) turn left through a metal kissing gate. Bear half-right through a large field, then walk beside the hedge to a kissing gate in the corner. Walk ahead up to the skyline in the next field then gently down beside the right-hand hedge/fence. At the bottom of the field turn right along a track and where this opens out into a field, bear left along the fence. At the end of the fence turn half-right in the direction of Malpas church passing to the right of a large pool to a kissing gate in the fence. Cut through the centre of the following field to a second kissing gate beside garages. Pass between the garages and houses and at the road turn left.

At the end of the road turn right, then left at the T junction to the main road. Turn right along the main road to the centre of Malpas and walk up 'High Street' returning to the car park to complete the walk.

*The size and isolation of Malpas today gives little idea of its past importance as the head manor of one of the largest baronies in Cheshire. It also formed the centre of Cheshire's largest parish and required several 'chapels of ease' for outlying areas (see notes on St. Chad's in the following chapter). These saved parishioners the long walk to Malpas Church.*

*Near the church lie the earthworks of a Norman motte and bailey castle, one of many along this troubled border with Wales. Today, the*

83

*village lies off the main road but in the Middle Ages it commanded one of the main routes north to Chester. This followed the line of the old Roman road which took a north-west line from Whitchurch passing through the sites of Malpas and Stretton, crossing the Dee at Aldford ('old ford') and continuing to Chester. The lanes between Tilston and Whitchurch still follow the line of this road.*

*The Cross, Malpas*

# Whitchurch

**Distance:** *9 miles.*

**Section of Sandstone Trail:** *Old St. Chad's Church to Whitchurch.*

**Start:** *Begin the walk at the 'Blue Bell Inn', an ancient half-timbered inn situated on a loop of the old A41 at Bell o' th' Hill, 3 miles north of Whitchurch. Park on a small piece of waste lane opposite the inn. Grid ref. 523 454 (Ordnance Survey Landranger 117, Explorer 257).*

**Local facilities:** *Whitchurch – local shops, pubs, cafés and post office. The 'Blue Bell Inn' at the start of the walk, 'Willeymoor Lock' on the canal and the 'Horse and Jockey' at Grindley Brook.*

## The walk

**1.** Facing the 'Blue Bell Inn' turn left along the lane. In about 350 yards turn right along a short track which leads to the main road (ignore a track before this which passes under the road). Cross the road (A41) and follow the lane opposite. Go through the right-hand gate at the end of the lane and cut through the field to the isolated church of Old St. Chad's.

*This ancient church, dedicated to Saint Chad, was built in 1689 and was in regular use until 1863 when a new church, also dedicated to St. Chad, was built nearby on the main road. As a result, the old church now lies stranded in the middle of fields and can only be approached on foot. The present building replaced a much older timber framed structure which may have contained parts dating from its earliest beginnings.*

*It was originally built as a 'chapel of ease' for the convenience of locals who were spared the long walk to Malpas, which lay at the centre*

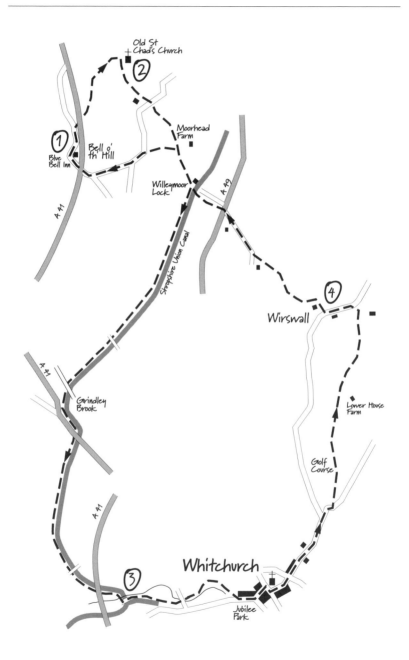

Old St
Chad's Church

②

Moorhead
Farm

①

Bell o'
th' Hill

Blue
Bell Inn

Willeymoor
Lock

A 41

A 49

Shropshire Union Canal

④

Wirswall

A 41

Grindley
Brook

Lower House
Farm

A 41

Golf
Course

③

Whitchurch

Jubilee
Park

*The 'Blue Bell Inn', Bell o' th' Hill*

of the largest medieval parish in Cheshire. Today Old St. Chad's still has a function as the parish burial ground as no cemetery exists at the new church and monthly services are still held here during the summer.

The small building to the left of the church was previously a meeting room but now houses an old horse drawn hearse built in 1880. It was last used in the 1920s and has now been restored.

The isolated location of the church may be explained by the antiquity of the site. In the intervening centuries the highway has shifted westwards to the present line taken by the A41. John Ogilby's 'Britanica', published in 1675, shows that in the seventeenth century the Whitchurch to Chester road passed much closer to Old St. Chad's, while Thomas Burdett's map of Cheshire published a century later, shows a minor road still passing close to the church.

*During the Middle Ages, when a church was first built here, most highways were based on Roman roads and only in the eighteenth century when the new turnpike roads were built, did any great change take place. These were built mainly for stage coaches and gradients were of great importance. Roman roads on the other hand, took the shortest distance between points, usually following straight lines and often ignored all but the steepest hillsides. Many of these ancient roads are now lost beneath the fields, although their approximate line can often be calculated with reasonable accuracy.*

**2.** Leave the cemetery by the gate and turn left to a stile a few yards away (or turn right as you approach if you do not visit the church). Continue straight ahead to a second stile at the bottom of the field. Walk directly ahead through the following field to a track beside a small farmhouse on the right. Bear left along the track for about 50 yards then bear left over a stile and through a small field to a quiet lane. Turn right along the lane for about 30 yards to a footbridge and kissing gate on the left. Go through the gate and keep to the right-hand field edges. Cross the access road to Moorhead Farm on the left and keep beside a fence to a stile ahead. Go over the stile and continue with the fence on your right to a second stile by a house over to the left. Cross the stile and go ahead to a kissing gate into fields again. Walk half-left through the field to a kissing gate to join the tow path on the Shropshire Union Canal beside the 'Willeymoor Lock' pub. Turn right and follow the tow path to 'Grindley Brook Lock', about 1$^{1}/_{2}$ miles (bridge number 29).

Continue along the towpath passing 'Danson's Bridge' (number 30) and beneath the bypass (number 30a).

**3.** Less than $^{1}/_{2}$ mile further on you come to a small lift bridge with a short arm of the canal on the left. Turn left over the bridge and walk along the towpath to the end of the canal arm (about 300 yards). Continue ahead on a new path to a road ('Greenfields Rise'). Bear diagonally-left across the road to continue on a footpath through a small valley with a stream (Red Brook) to

*Lift bridge on the approach to Whitchurch*

your right. Near houses up to the left, continue ahead ignoring a footpath on the left. At a road turning area, keep ahead down a track passing a house on the left to eventually reach a road— 'Waterside Close'. Turn left then immediately left again.

Across the road on the right is Jubilee Park where the *Sandstone Trail* ends. To continue on the circular walk follow the road up to a mini roundabout and bear left. Walk towards the church and at a second mini roundabout immediately before the church turn right, then left at the 'The Black Bear'.

*The history of Whitchurch reaches back to the Roman period when it was known as Mediolanum. Its small timber fort is thought to have been used as a halt by legions marching north to Deva (Chester), about 20 miles and a day's march away. Before the Norman Conquest the Lordship was owned by King Harold and was later mentioned in the Domesday Book as 'Westune'.*

*Whitchurch was the home of Sir John Talbot (1373 – 1453), a notable English general and knight. He rose to prominence as the first Earl of Shrewsbury and was twice Governor of Ireland, but he remained an enthusiastic campaigner throughout his life meeting his end at the Battle of Castillon at the age of 80!*

*Today Whitchurch is a quiet country town with lots of inviting pubs and numerous old buildings from the Georgian period.*

Pass the 'Horse and Jockey' and continue ahead along 'Claypit Street' to the main road. Take the road ahead (still 'Claypit Street') which soon becomes 'Alport Road'. At a fork, with the road to the left signed to 'Wirswall', keep ahead for about 200 yards to a signed footpath on the left. The next section crosses the golf course and the line of the right of way is not waymarked (at the time of writing) and can be hard to follow. The approximate line is due north. (Alternatively, you can avoid this section by turning left along the lane signed to 'Wirswall' 200 yards back. For this option follow the lane to Wirswall and continue from point 4.)

After the stile bear half-right across the golf course, shortly passing a green on your left. Take a direct line from here passing a tiny pond beside a willow tree on the right before rising steeply up a bank. Pass a second green (no. 15) on the left and at a belt of small conifers bear left along a gravel path. As the ground begins to drop bear right through the trees, cross a fairway and walk down hill to a large tree at the outside corner of a field on the right. Bear half-right veering away from the hedge on your right. Make a rise again to pass tee no. 18 on your right. There is a pond ahead here—turn right now then swing left to a stile below a power line post.

Go over the stile and cut directly through the rising field crossing a farm track to a stile in the far hedge. Bear diagonally-left to a stile in the far corner and continue on the same line in the next field to a stile in the far hedge. Keep beside the hedge on the left to a gate in the corner. Go through the gate and bear half-left along the hedge to another gate. Go ahead through the centre of the field in the direction of a large mast. A stile in a fence leads onto an access track. Go over the stile and turn left to the lane. Turn left and walk along the lane for about 300 yards to the handful of houses and farms at Wirswall.

**4.** Take the signed bridleway (an unsurfaced access road immediately before 'The Paddocks') on the right (on the left if you have taken the lane option instead of the golf course). Walk past 'The Spinney' and turn left as signed immediately after the garden. Follow this path between hedges to eventually join another green lane. Turn right here as signed and follow the track between fields until it swings right (can be muddy). Keep ahead on a footpath to reach an access road lower down. Follow the road ahead down to the busy A49.

Turn right for a few yards, then cross over and take the signed footpath through a field immediately before the driveway to 'Willeymoor Lock'. Cross a footbridge and the locks to the far towpath beside the pub and turn left. In a few yards take the signed footpath on the right. Retrace the outward route to the track to Moorhead Farm on the right and turn left down the track to join a quiet lane. Turn left along the lane. At the top of the rise keep right at a T junction, cross the A41 and follow the lane opposite back to the 'Blue Bell Inn'.

# Mara Books www.marabooks.co.uk

Mara Books publish a range of walking books for Cheshire and North Wales and have the following list to date.

## North Wales

### Circular Walks in the Conwy Valley

ISBN 0 9522409 7 1. A collection of 18 circular walks which explore the varied scenery of this beautiful valley from the Great Orme to Betws-y-Coed.

### Walking in Snowdonia Volume 1

ISBN 1 902512 06 5. A series of circular walks exploring the beautiful and dramatic valleys in the northern half of the Snowdonia National Park.

### A pocket guide to Snowdon

ISBN 1 902512 04 9. A guide to all Snowdon's recognised routes of ascent, from the six 'Classic Paths' to the many lesser known and less frequented routes.

### Coastal Walks around Anglesey Volume 1

ISBN 0 9522409 6 3. A collection of 15 walks which explore the varied scenery of Anglesey's beautiful coastline.

### Coastal Walks around Anglesey Volume 2

ISBN 0 9522409 5 5. A companion volume to the above book, outlining 15 new walks spread around Anglesey's fascinating and beautiful coastline.

### Walking the Isle of Anglesey Coastal Path

ISBN 1 902512 13 8. The official guide for the Isle of Anglesey Coastal Path. Full colour in English and Welsh.

## Walking on the Lleyn Peninsula

ISBN 1 902512 00 6. A collection of 16 circular walks which explore the wild and beautiful coastline and hills of the Lleyn Peninsula.

## Walking in the Clwydian Hills

ISBN 1 902512 09 X. A collection of 18 circular walks exploring the Clwydian Range Area of Outstanding Natural Beauty (AONB).

## Walking in the Vale of Clwyd and Denbigh Moors

ISBN 1 902512 08 1. A collection of 18 circular walks exploring the undiscovered country between the Clwydian Hills and the Conwy Valley.

## Circular walks along the Offa's Dyke Path

### —Volume 1 Prestatyn to Welshpool
ISBN 1 902512 01 4.

### —Volume 2 Welshpool to Hay-on-Wye
ISBN 1 902512 07 3.

The first two volumes in a series of three which sample some of the finest sections of this well known national trail.

## The Mountain Men

ISBN 1 902512 11 1. This book tells the story of the pioneer rock climbers in Snowdonia in the closing decades of the nineteenth century until the outbreak of World War II.

# Cheshire

### Circular Walks along the Gritstone Trail and Mow Cop Trail

ISBN 0 9522409 4 7. A route which follows Cheshire's eastern border along the edge of the Peak District. Following the same format as the Sandstone Trail book—a full description for both trails is combined with 12 circular walks.

### A Walker's Guide to the Wirral Shore Way

ISBN 1 902512 05 7. A linear walk of 23 miles following the old coastline between Chester and Hoylake.

### Circular Walks in Wirral

ISBN 1 902512 02 2. A collection of 15 circular walks in the coast and countryside of Wirral.

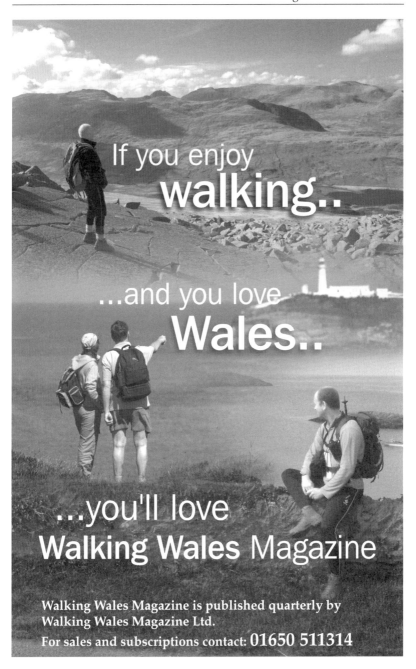